RECLAIMING EVANGELISM

RECLAIMING EVANGELISM

A PRACTICAL GUIDE
FOR MAINLINE CHURCHES

Jan G. Linn

Chalice Press
St. Louis, Missouri

All scripture quotations, unless otherwise indicated, are from the New Revised Standard Version Bible, copyright 1989, Division of Christian Education of the National Council of the Churches of Christ in the USA. Used by permission.

Cover design: Cecil King

This book is printed on acid-free, recycled paper.

Visit Chalice Press on the World Wide Web at
http://www.chalicepress.com

10 9 8 7 6 5 4 3 2 1   98 99 00 01 02 03

Library of Congress Cataloging–in–Publication Data

Linn, Jan.
    Reclaiming evangelism: a guide for mainline churches / by Jan G. Linn.
      p. cm.
    Includes bibliographical references.
    ISBN 0-8272-3216-0
    1. Evangelistic work—Philosophy. 2. Evangelistic work—United States. 3. Liberalism (Religion)—Protestant churches. 4. Liberalism (Religion)—United States. 5. United States—Church history—20th century. I. Title.
BV3793.L5   1998   97-44095
269'.1—dc21   CIP

Printed in the United States of America

Acknowledgments

An author cannot be sure if persons acknowledged for their help or influence consider it a tribute or a bit of an embarrassment. This is especially true when the subject is one about which perspectives can be both widely divergent and passionately held, as in the case of evangelism. So let me say first that the persons to whom I owe much gratitude for reading all or parts of this book did the best they could to improve upon it. Its strengths can be attributed to their helpful criticisms, whereas its weaknesses are solely of my doing. I want to publicly thank Sally Burgess, Michael Kinnamon, David Hartman, Ruth Kitchen, Bob Hill, Tom Russell, and Greg Alexander. My thanks also to an ecumenical group of Kansas ministers for the hospitality and stimulating discussion we had on parts of the book—Sara Blodgett, Keith Dellenbach, Wayne Schabaugh, Kim Rae, Greg Rae, Bill Boyle, Matt Keith, John Lauenberg, John Park Winkler, Lois Lougee, Bob Weitzel, and especially Lee Parker, who was the convener.

Sincere appreciation must be expressed to the members of the Board of Trustees of Lexington Theological Seminary for their support of the generous sabbatical program that undergirds faculty research and writing. This book is a direct result of having spent an entire academic year completing the research and a first draft on this important subject in the life of the church. During this time the library staff at Central Baptist Theological Seminary in Kansas City, Kansas, extended faculty privileges to me, for which I am most grateful. I especially want to thank Ann Jeffries for her specific assistance on more than a few occasions, and most especially for her attitude, so obviously pleasant that I felt immediately at home in unfamiliar surroundings.

During sabbatical my wife and I were able to do ministry with two congregations, First Christian Church, Mayfield, Kentucky, for two months, and Fairview Christian Church, Kansas City, Missouri, for nine months. To these congregations, and especially to their pastors, Glenn Evans and Loyd Gentry, respectively, we express heartfelt appreciation for opportunities to have fresh experience in congregational ministry. We shall always remember the loving spirit overflowing from these wonderful congregations.

The person who deserves the most credit for any contribution to the life of the church this book might make, and absolution of any responsibility for its shortcomings, is my wife, Joy. The long and short of it is that this book would never have been completed had it not been for her willingness to read endless drafts and her patience in supporting the hours I took from our life together to write. It was no surprise that her genuine enthusiasm for the book was exceeded only by the obvious delight visible on her face when I announced that at long last it was done.

Finally, I want to thank David Polk at Chalice Press, not only for his support of this project before the first page was written, but for the years we have worked together in this ministry of writing that is one of the ways I am able to witness to the hope that is within me.

Contents

Introduction

This book is about evangelism. Specifically, it is about evangelism and mainline churches.[1] It naturally follows my previous book, entitled *The Jesus Connection: A Christian Spirituality*.[2] Describing a spirituality in the church that is peculiarly "Christian," that book focused on Christians being "connected" to Jesus. It is this "connectedness" that constitutes the cornerstone of the church's ministry of evangelism. In a real sense, evangelism is passionate spirituality unbridled.

I began this work fully aware that some people consider mainline evangelism an oxymoron. They see mainline churches as having given up on evangelism a long time ago, with dramatic membership decline to prove it. I would admit that there is an element of truth to the charge. There are exceptions, of course, but on the whole evangelism has not been a major focus in mainline church life in the last thirty-five-plus years. One never knows which is the chicken and which is the egg, so to speak, but this neglect was in part either caused by or the result of evangelism's becoming identified with those who stand on the theological right, especially of the fundamentalist stripe. Consequently, justice-seeking became the missionary focus among mainliners. It is a bit ironic, though, that mainliners have worked for justice in the name of faithfulness to the gospel, yet have neglected the ministry of evangelism that lies at the heart of that faithfulness. This book argues for a change, for mainline churches reclaiming this ministry precisely because being faithful to the gospel demands it.

At the same time, mainline suspicions about the way non-mainliners understand and practice evangelism also need to

1

be taken seriously. No significant reclaiming of this ministry is likely without a thorough reexamination of its theology and practice. Consequently, this book explores both what evangelism is and what it is not. Let me summarize the chapters that follow.

The church is called to be in the world, but not of it. Chapter 1 describes the "world" mainline churches are in by assessing the relationship between church and culture in the American context. I try to show that the role of the church today is very different, in fact, permanently different, than it was in the United States of yesterday. At the same time I argue that even in the face of constant change things are amazingly similar to the environment the church faced in the first century, which makes the ministry of evangelism as relevant now as it was then.

Chapter 2 arises out of the conviction that the first priority regarding the ministry of evangelism is for the church to be committed to theology guiding methodology. Unfortunately, just the opposite exists now, which accounts for marketing strategies that undercut the very meaning of Christian discipleship. This chapter focuses on a theological foundation for evangelism. The argument advanced centers on a Christian soteriology (doctrine of salvation) that boldly affirms faith in God's gift of salvation in Jesus Christ but abandons the traditional Christian triumphalism that forces the validity of Christianity to be dependent upon the invalidity of all other religious claims. In an effort to speak to laity as well as clergy, I have sought to make the chapter as "reader friendly" as possible.

The meaning, purpose, and shape of evangelism are the focuses of Chapter 3. Here I argue for mainline churches to reclaim this ministry as found in the New Testament's call for intentional witnessing. It invites churches to become conscious of ways they can name the name of Jesus as Savior and Lord in all aspects of their corporate life. Further, I argue that evangelism is not something a church *does*. It is something a church *is* because it is an outward manifestation of an inward reality. In other words, I seek to show that evangelism is rooted in genuine spirituality.

Chapters 4 and 5 should be understood as two parts of a whole. Spiritual stagnation is the primary obstacle to mainline churches' engaging in evangelism. Chapter 4 explains why this is the case and offers a number of practical steps churches can take to confront it. Chapter 6 consists of an extended and detailed description of how mainline churches can reorganize themselves in order to do the ministry of evangelism. Moving off dead center and into a renewal of life and ministry requires restructuring congregations. If anything in the earlier chapters offers help to mainline churches, then the call for restructuring church life must be taken seriously.

Chapter 6 confronts one of the troubling realities when the subject of evangelism comes up. In most churches the bottom line is membership growth. This has become both the goal and chief measure of effective evangelism. The influence of the church growth movement is dominant. Swimming against a strong current, through a careful study of the Great Commission, I try to make the case that the merging of evangelism and church growth is an unholy alliance. At the same time, recognizing that many mainline churches have acted naively about the effects of numerical decline, and wanting to challenge their complacency about evangelism, I offer a way for churches to think about numerical growth without making it their primary aim or measure of success.

I also invite readers to pay attention to the notes at the end of each chapter. They serve an important function for anyone wanting to engage this discussion of evangelism in greater depth. Beyond appropriate identification of cited references, this material expands the discussion by addressing issues raised by the main text, but tangential to it. Part of what I have tried to do in the notes is to anticipate questions my views on evangelism might raise.

In the end I hope this book will be seen as an effort to speak words of encouragement to mainline churches and ministers. Worried and anxious because of numerical decline, tense and tentative in trying to cope with controversial theological issues, mainliners are a worn-out people. We need some new life. That will happen, I believe, as we regain confidence in seeking to be faithful in ministry and at the same time witness to the the true Source of new life, new life that transcends temporal ups and downs. I hope this book will make a contribution to this end.

NOTES

[1] Perhaps, as Wade Clark Roof and William McKinney suggest, the appropriate term is "old mainline" (*American Mainline Religion* [New Brunswick: Rutgers University Press, 1987], p. 233). I am referring specifically to those predominantly white churches of the Protestant establishment that include the American Baptists, Presbyterians, United Methodists, Episcopalians, Lutherans, United Church of Christ, Christian Church (Disciples of Christ), and the Reformed Church of America. For a detailed mapping of mainline Protestantism, see the chapter in Roof and McKinney entitled "The Fragmented Mainline" (pp. 72–105).

[2] St. Louis: Chalice Press, 1997.

The "World" Mainline Churches Are in Today: We've Been Here Before

I want to begin with what appear to be two contradictory observations that provide the context for our discussion. The first is that everything has changed in the church, to paraphrase Einstein's observation at the dawn of the nuclear age, except our modes of thinking. The great scientist went on to say, "Thus, we drift toward unparalleled catastrophes."[1] I won't go that far, but I am convinced that everything has changed in and for the church today. The second observation is that the more things change, the more they stay the same. Let me expand on each of these.

People in general, and church folk in particular, often use the metaphor of a swinging pendulum to describe change. Change is little more than a pendulum swing from one side to the other. Whichever way the pendulum has previously swung, it will eventually move back in the opposite direction. All we have to do is to wait, or endure, as the case may be, until it happens. And in fact there are times when the metaphor seems very accurate. For example, a focus on personal responsibility has certainly made a comeback in the political rhetoric of this country in the last five years. An often used phrase these days is "Opportunity for all and responsibility from all." It is a theme whose currency has become negotiable once again in the popular political market-place. Yet, the conviction that people need to take responsibility for themselves, at times needing a hand up, but never a handout, is an old, pre-Depression and pre-"Great Society" theme. That it is making a comeback points to a pendulum swing.

We see a similar pattern regarding the role of government. The popular notion that epitomized the Reagan years of the '80s that the best government governs least, with the ideal government governing not at all,[2] is now giving way to a measure of support even among staunch conservatives for the appropriate role of government in areas such as education, protection of the environment, and worker-friendly laws such as the Family Leave Act. Conservative voices have even been heard cautioning conservative colleagues not to rush to dismantle affirmative action legislation.[3] Here, again, a pendulum swing is an appropriate metaphor for change.

Pendulum swings are found in all areas of human endeavor, perhaps nowhere more frequently than the fashion industry. I have a closetful of old neckties I recycle from year to year, depending upon which way the style pendulum has swung. Trends come and go in businesses, social customs, and even religion. Yet, there are times when the pendulum metaphor fails to capture the permanency of the effects of change. There are periods where events have a revolutionary impact on a society. The discovery of bronze was such a moment, as was the discovery of iron. The industrial revolution was another, the splitting of the atom yet another. So, too, with the technological advances that led to the U.S. putting a man on the moon. Epochal moments mark the dawn of a new day wherein the pendulum itself requires recalibrating. Bill Gates, co-founder and chairman of Microsoft, suggests that the information age we are now in is a similar epochal moment.[4] I believe he is correct. The speed

of and access to information that computers have made possible have changed everything, this time including our modes
of thinking. The information age has increased our sense of
the rapidity of change. The news of the successful cloning of
sheep in Scotland had an immediate impact on the world.

Change, especially the "epochal moment" kind of change,
creates internal as well as external upheaval. Attitudes, values, and behavior are altered, affecting all societal institutions, including, and for our purposes, especially, the church.
Consider the following examples of the attitudinal changes
toward the church and its place in society that have occurred
in the last thirty years:

- 11:00 Sunday morning is no longer a sacred hour
  for worship, but a time of work and recreation for
  millions of Americans.

- What the church says is right and wrong is tested
  or rejected by post–World War II generations suspi-
  cious of all authority.

- The basis for involvement in the church by the
  young who are interested enough to take it seriously
  is a marketplace mentality rather than family or denominational loyalty.

- A widespread acceptance of religious pluralism increases the pressure on the church to accept the fact
  that it is no longer the only major league team on
  the religious playing field.

All of these changes point up the fact that the church in
America today exists in a society that is not only different
from yesterday's, but is permanently different. Moreover,
these changes reflect not only a sidelining of mainline
churches, but in many ways the whole of Christianity. Christians must come to grips with the fact that no pendulum
swing signaling a return to the days when the church determined the ethos of a community's life is likely to occur again.

As a consequence, the influence of the Christian community on the values and ethics of the larger society has diminished significantly. While the larger society is not completely devoid of religious values, ours is nonetheless a time when secularism is dominant. The consensus around national values, beliefs, and customs that was rooted in the Judeo-Christian heritage and carried the name "civil religion" began to crumble in the sixties. Though some see a resurgence of religion in the secular city,[5] the prevailing view is that "secular" is an appropriate description of the current climate in this country.[6]

Moreover, some observers go another step and suggest that religion in general, and Christianity in particular, are gradually being placed in a defensive posture. Yale law professor Stephen Carter believes segments of American society, arrogant in their insistence on an impermeable barrier between church and state, not only ignore the church but go a step further and trivialize the importance of religion in American society. Says Carter, "One sees a trend in our political and legal cultures toward treating religious beliefs as arbitrary and unimportant, a trend supported by a rhetoric that implies there is something wrong with religious devotion."[7] Catholic scholar Richard John Neuhaus recognizes hostility toward religion in what he calls "the public square," but he is persuaded that such overt hostility "is no longer in good taste because it is no longer necessary. Rather than attacking religion, cultural elites quietly assume its irrelevance."[8]

The church is directly affected by this negative attitude toward religious devotion. Kennon Callahan argues that "the day of the churched culture is over. The day of the mission field has come."[9] He means by this that the day when the church's voice and role in the larger society were respected ("a churched culture") has given way to a culture that is now the mission field for the church. He believes ministers and laity together must see themselves as a mission team much like "a M*A*S*H unit that moves flexibly and quickly to where the needs are, close to the front lines" of human hurts

and hopes.[10] Sociologist Robert Wuthnow, while arguing for
the importance of a continuing role of the church, as well as
denominations, in American society into the twenty-first century, nonetheless acknowledges the "sidelined" position in
which mainline churches find themselves.[11]

A voice from the culture itself assesses the position of the
church today in very much the same way. Writer/producer
Norman Lear has written:

> We are living through a wrenching transition—eco-
> nomically, culturally, spiritually. The old certainties
> are gone, and the new ones have yet to crystallize.
> We need only think back a generation or two to see
> how much has changed. The institutions of the
> church, the family, education and civil authority—
> the world that Walter Lippman referred to as "that
> old ancestral order"—no longer command the same
> authority or respect. Once responsible for purveying
> values from one generation to another, and for giv-
> ing a deep sense of order, continuity, and higher
> meaning to our culture, now these institutions are
> beleaguered and divided.[12]

I recently had a conversation that illustrated for me the
reality of the sidelining of Christianity in modern society.
On a recent flight I was sitting beside a young woman who
is a neurologist doing research at a major university in the
South. She grew up in Texas, attended a Christian school
through high school, then attended college and medical
school in New York. Soon after the plane took off she re-
trieved a copy of Jack Miles' best-selling book *God: A Biography*[13] from her bag and began to read. Curious about her
choice of reading material, I risked engaging her in conversation. She responded pleasantly enough to indicate she
didn't mind. As we talked I was struck by her knowledge of
the Bible. It was in response to my asking her how she came
by this knowledge that she told me her background, a background in which the church had played a significant role. By

the end of the conversation I was comfortable enough to ask her if she still attended church. She said no, that at the moment she was more interested in Islam than Christianity. When pressed as to why she had abandoned the church, she replied that it just didn't hold her interest any longer.

This young woman is not alone. The church does not hold interest for a lot of people today, and it seems mainline churches are least able to hold anybody's interest.[14] If one were to believe the statistical conclusions of church consultants and pollsters, mainline churches are pretty much finished.[15] But the truth is, this kind of statistical data is simply verification of what every pastor and church member in a mainline congregation has known for a long time. Everybody knows mainline churches are in trouble numerically, but what is not commonly understood is that the reasons are anything but simple. Some factors contributing to their decline are in fact independent of what mainliners do or don't do. Donald Luidens writes, "While explanations for the aggregate decline are not simple, one guiding principle should be kept in mind: these losses are the result of large-scale social and cultural forces virtually impervious to churchly control—although they are always subject to Christian critique."[16]

Whatever the reasons, though, the effects of numerical decline have been significant. An important one has been the loss of an influential voice in the public arena. Numerically declining institutions don't have much influence. Local, state, and national public leaders pay little attention to mainline views on issues of today, while presidents and presidential candidates accept invitations to speak at gatherings of the religious right. President Clinton is the only President in modern times to invite leaders from mainline churches to meetings at the White House in cooperation with the National Council of Churches, but even with that the press calls non-mainline ministers Bill Hybels and Robert Schuller "the President's ministers," and for good reason. Schuller has been seen sitting with the First Family during State of the Union addresses, and Bill Hybels has had regular meetings with Clinton during and after the '96 campaign.[17] Politicians in general do not view mainline church leaders as a formidable force in elections, and choose, instead, to reach out to Christian Right groups such as the Christian Coalition.

Another effect of numerical decline is that mainline church membership has become vulnerable to the influence of an inverted deteuronomic ethic. It is a common malady in tough times. The book of Deuteronomy describes the relationship of God to Israel as an ethic of blessings and curses. God will bless Israel in the land of promise if the people follow Torah and curse Israel if the people reject Torah. When this ethic of blessings and curses is inverted, it leads to the conclusion that when one is prospering, God must be offering a blessing, but if one is faltering or suffering, God is not offering a blessing. In short, one who falters or suffers must be doing something wrong. An indication that this inversion is at work in mainline churches is the often-asked question "Why are 'those other churches' growing and we're not?" With the predictable appendage, "They must be doing something right" (and we must be doing something wrong).

Mainline churches have been significantly influenced by this way of thinking, whether we are conscious of it or not. There has been a predictable negative impact on our membership as a result. At the moment mainline churches are discouraged and dispirited. We occasionally grumble at the church growth folk, in some instances try to copy them, and in our most discouraging moments, envy them. We are frustrated and angry at ourselves and among ourselves. Self-flagellation and collegial criticism have become common. Relationships between denominational leaders and congregational pastors are at best tense, and sometimes downright hostile.

Yet in spite of the sidelining of mainline churches, I believe we are living at a "kairotic" moment in mainline church life, a moment ripe for a recovery of the ministry of evangelism. I say this because of the second observation made earlier, that the more things change, the more they stay the same. Two things lead me to this conclusion. The first is that the culture in which Christianity finds itself at the end of the twentieth century in America is very much like the culture the church faced at the end of the first century. In his book *How To Reach Secular People*, George Hunter identifies four objectives of the early Christian proclamation of the gospel that describe the world as it was then. First, facing a population with no knowledge of the gospel, the Christian movement had to *inform* people of Jesus, the good news, its claims, and its offer. Second, facing a hostile population and persecution from the state, the church had to win friends and *influence* people. Third, facing an empire with several entrenched religions, Christians had to *convince* people of Christianity's truth, or at least its plausibility. Fourth, since entry into the faith is an act of the will, Christians had to *invite* people to adopt this faith and join the messianic community and follow Jesus as Lord.[18]

Arguing that today's world is a secular one, Hunter relies on the work of Martin Marty to describe three forms the schism between the church and Western culture has taken: (1) utter secularity, which involves an attack on God and the church; (2) mere secularity, meaning the church and God are ignored; and (3) controlled secularity, characterized by civil religion, or the use of Christian symbols whose meanings have been changed.[19] These forms, coupled with Hunter's analysis of the context of first-century church life, suggest significant similarities to the environment in which the church today lives after twenty centuries of change. In short, the church has been here before.[20]

The second reason for suggesting that the more things change, the more they stay the same is the fact that the internal upheaval change creates only exacerbates a basic human need for contact with spiritual things. In his book *The Politics of Meaning*, psychologist Michael Lerner says the basic and pervasive problem in America today is a loss of meaning. Based upon research he and colleagues conducted among middle-income people in Oakland, California, in the mid-seventies, Lerner came to the conclusion that most Americans are desperate for hope. He writes:

> We hunger to be recognized by others, to be cherished for our own sakes and not for what we have accomplished or possess, and to be acknowledged as people who care about something higher and more important than our own self-interest. We hunger also for communities of meaning that can transcend the individualism and selfishness that we see around us and that will provide an ethical and spiritual framework that gives our lives some higher purposes.[21]

Lerner critiques the inadequacies of both conservatives and liberals in seeking to provide a politics of meaning today, in part because even with their different agendas, neither poses any real challenge to the individualism and materialism that reign as the gods of American consumerism. He argues that if we commit ourselves as a nation to working for the common good, we can put *compassion* at the center of our collective life. It is compassion, he says, that is "the central element" in a meaning-oriented society.[22]

Lerner's critics argue that he tempts us with an idealism that offers little in terms of real power to change the dominant culture,[23] or that he speaks to a problem that is for the most part a middle- and upper-class problem. But I would argue that meaning-making knows no economic class, that in fact the search for meaning, along with the need for belonging, is a universal need. More important, it is to both of these needs that the gospel speaks persuasively. Offering hope to people hungering for meaning and belonging has always been at the heart of the Christian message. Though secularity may rule the day externally, Lerner's work suggests that its failure to satisfy the deepest need of the human soul makes a ministry of evangelism both relevant and urgent. A sidelined church faces the challenge to become a bold witness to the gospel it believes makes meaning possible.[24]

These two propositions, then, describe the context for a ministry of evangelism in mainline churches. Everything has changed in the world as we know it today, and we need to come to grips with this reality without wasting time waiting for the pendulum to swing back to yesterday. It isn't going to happen, and those who wait for it will eventually discover they have been left behind because they were unprepared for the present, not unlike the bridesmaids in Jesus' parable who were caught without oil for their lamps (Matthew 25:1–12). At the same time, the more things change, the more they stay the same. In the information age, where change seems the only constant, the gospel has never been more relevant simply because, in the midst of change, the primary spiritual need of human beings in the twentieth century is no different from that in the first. Change does not give meaning to life. Nor does information necessarily tell us what ultimately matters. It comes down to the quality of change and the way in which information is used. Both of these have to do with values that help the human spirit know there is something beyond the moment that has ultimate value, that there is a transcendent dimension to life. In the church we call this spirituality. At a time when people still hunger for meaning, for belonging, for a sense that their lives count for something beyond the moment, the ministry of evangelism seems as urgent as it ever was. Perhaps more important, the church believes in a gospel that demands it.

NOTES

[1] As quoted in Jonathan Schell, *The Fate of the Earth* (New York: Alfred A. Knopf, 1982), p. 188.

[2] This popular phrase comes from Thoreau's essay, "Civil Disobedience," in which he went on to say, "That government is best which governs not at all," but the caveat most often overlooked today is that Thoreau added the stipulation that "when men are prepared for it, that will be the kind of government which they will have." *Walden and Other Writings of Henry David Thoreau*, ed. Brooks Atkinson (New York: The Modern Library, 1950), p. 635.

[3] Speaker of the House Newt Gingrich, congressman from Georgia, was reported in the *Kansas City Star*, April 14, 1997, p. A-9, as making this plea.

[4] Bill Gates, *The Road Ahead* (New York: Viking Press, 1995).

[5] Harvey Cox, *Religion in The Secular City* (New York: Simon & Schuster, 1994).

[6] Roof and McKinney, pp. 8–9.

[7] Stephen L. Carter, *The Culture of Disbelief* (New York: Anchor Books, 1993), p. 6.

[8] Richard John Neuhaus, *The Naked Public Square*, 2nd ed. (Grand Rapids: Eerdmans, 1984), p. 95. Though courts, secular historians, and social theorists assert that "religion cannot provide the cohesion required" in a secular society, Newhaus does not believe they speak for the majority of average citizens (ibid.).

[9] Kennon L. Callahan, *Effective Church Leadership: Building on the Twelve Keys* (San Francisco: Harper & Row, 1990), p. 13.

[10] Ibid., p. 28.

[11] Robert Wuthnow, *Christianity in the 21st Century* (New York: Oxford University Press, 1993). Wuthnow argues that Christians' having a place in the next century will depend on "the ways in which the church meets the cultural challenges it faces" (p. 31). He says mainliners have been sidelined primarily by letting fundamentalists set the public religious agenda (ch. 9).

[12] Norman Lear, "Confessions of an Unaffiliated Groper," *Noetic Sciences Review* (Autumn, 1996), p. 6.

[13] Jack Miles, *God: A Biography* (New York: Vintage Books, 1996).

[14] According to the Gallup Organization and the Princeton Religious Research Center, weekly worship attendance here in the U.S. dropped in 1996 to 38 percent of the adult population, one percent above the lowest recorded since 1940, and down from 43 percent in 1995. Cited in a *Kansas City Star* editorial, April 27, 1997.

[15] See George Barna, *Successful Churches: What They Have in Common* (Glendale: the Barna Research Group, 1990). Barna claims that most churches in America are either in a state of numerical stagnation or decline, with mainline churches leading the way (p. 1). Lyle Schaller, *Innovations in Ministry: Models for The 21st Century* (Nashville: Abingdon, 1994, p. 52), and Ben Campbell Johnson, *Rethinking Evangelism: A Theological Mandate* (Philadelphia: The Westminster Press, 1987, p. 13) make similar claims.

[16] Donald Luidens, "Fighting 'decline': Mainline churches and the tyranny of aggregate data," *The Christian Century*, November 6, 1996, p. 1075. See also Luidens' work with Ben R. Hoge and Benton Johnson, *Vanishing Boundaries: The Religion of Mainline Protestant Baby Boomers* (Louisville: Westminster John Knox, 1994). These authors researched various categories of baby boomer Presbyterians regarding their reasons for attending and dropping out of Presbyterian church life. Their findings verify the complexity of mainline decline. They finally conclude that Dean Kelley (*Why Conservative Churches Are Growing*, New York: Harper & Row, 1972)

was correct in his thesis that meaning-making is a primary factor in growth, while a certain amount of decline is endemic to institutional perpetuity. Their research also challenges the persistent charge that engagement in social action and controversial issues in lieu of a commitment to evangelism is another reason for mainline church decline. See as well the authors' article entitled "Mainline Churches: The Real Reason for Decline" (*First Things*, March, 1993), in which they call on mainline churches that want to be renewed to begin addressing questions of faith that informed people today are asking.

[17] Robert Schuller is the founder of the Crystal Cathedral in Orange County, California, which broadcasts its weekly worship service across the nation. Bill Hybels is the founder of Willow Creek Community Church near Chicago, which has more than 16,000 people attending its various weekly worship services.

[18] George Hunter III, *How To Reach Secular People* (Nashville: Abingdon, 1992), p. 35.

[19] Ibid., p. 31.

[20] As will become obvious, however, I do not agree with Hunter's definition of evangelism as "the making of new Christian disciples," nor with his commitment to church growth evangelism more evident in his earlier book *The Contagious Congregation: Frontiers in Evangelism and Church Growth* (Nashville: Abingdon Press, 1979).

[21] Michael Lerner, *The Politics of Meaning* (New York: Addison-Wesley Publishing Co., 1996), p. 4.

[22] Ibid., pp. 156, 226.

[23] See Robert Westbrook's review, "Michael Lerner: The politics of meaning and the meaning of politics," *The Christian Century*, October 30, 1996, p. 1038.

[24] Wuthnow (Christianity in the 21st Century) says mainline churches must continue their historic role of creating communities of meaning that confer identity, support, and ethical direction (pp. 32–54). Moreover, the research of the authors of *Vanishing Boundaries* (see Note 16 above) adds an urgency to this ministry. Basing their conclusions on surveys and interviews with Presbyterian baby boomers, the authors found that helping people make sense and meaning of life remains a critical factor in their involvement in the church. Part of this task involves integrating the young into what Peter Berger calls "plausibility structures," or patterns of belief and practice that provide meaning to life.

2

Evangelism and Salvation in Jesus Christ

There are signs that mainline churches today are ready to take evangelism seriously, although in the face of the decline in membership this interest might be likened to a kind of "deathbed" conversion. Conferences sponsored by mainline churches, denominations, and seminaries on the subject are becoming more frequent, with clergy attendance on the increase. Perhaps what is happening is that mainliners are being forced to do some soul-searching about the nature and mission of the church. If this be the case, then embracing the ministry of evangelism as core to who we are becomes a real possibility.

But before we go running off to evangelize the world, we need to pause long enough to reflect theologically about this ministry. At the present time those churches that are concerned about evangelism are driven more by methodology than by theology. The implication is that we already know what evangelism is and need only to know how to do it effectively. "We spend too much time talking about it," one person said to me, "and too little time doing it. Tell us how

to do it, not what it is." This is a rather widespread senti-
ment. And, of course, methodology has its place, but when
it shapes theology, rather than the reverse, the confusion,
tension, and neglect of evangelism so commonplace today
among mainline churches is the inevitable result.[1]

There is, of course, the opposite extreme in mainline life,
a kind of radical but sterile liberalism that represents an
extreme theological relativism that cannot evangelize because
it will not affirm Jesus Christ as the cornerstone of faith. At
best, radical liberalism considers evangelism a tool for
Christian exclusivism that lacks sensitivity to other religious
traditions. At worst, it sees evangelism as an expression of a
naive understanding of the New Testament that has led
Christians to "tribalize" God in an effort to make God belong
only to them. From their perspective, Jesus was a teacher
who may have set an example for others to follow. Traditional
church doctrine, however, that claims anything decisive or
unique about his life, death, and resurrection needs a
revisionist perspective to make it palatable to the modern
mind. In between these extremes on the right and the left are,
I believe, the vast majority of mainline Christians, who believe
Jesus Christ is the Son of God but need to understand what
that means in the context of the reality of religious pluralism
they are not willing to ignore. I think most mainline ministers,
especially, find themselves in this in-between group. For years
caught in the widening schism between the church and the
academy, many of them are adrift in a crisis of authority and
even faith because of an education that taught them how to
take the Bible apart with the tools of higher critical study but
failed to teach them how to put it back together again. Though
there have been voices within the academy naming "the
broken promise of critical method,"[2] their pleas for help have
gone mostly unheeded by seminaries more committed to
credibility in the guild than service to the church. For this
majority, any theological foundation for the ministry of
witness evangelism must help answer the prophetic question
Dietrich Bonhoeffer asked years ago, "How [can we] live as

Christians in the modern world?" More to the point, how can we be "Christian," i.e., disciples of Jesus Christ, in a way that takes the particularity of Jesus Christ seriously, while rejecting Christian exclusivism? Is there a place to stand that frees Christians to witness to salvation in Jesus Christ without an out-of-hand condemnation of all non-Christians to hell?

Most mainline Christians have become at least vaguely familiar with other religious traditions in recent years. Their children have friends who are Jewish, Moslem, or Buddhist, or are no religion at all. The writings of non-Christians such as Elie Weisel and the lives of leaders like Gandhi have helped them to see both the worst side of Christian exclusivism and the best side of non-Christian religious conviction. I believe mainliners have reached what can be considered a level of healthy self-criticism that no longer ignores the ugly side of church history. They know about the senselessness of the crusades, the Spanish Inquisition, the centuries of anti-Semitism that sowed the seeds of the Holocaust, the nurturing of a "righteous empire" mentality that justified destroying native American life and much of its culture, and support of state-sponsored racism and segregation here in the United States and in South Africa. They also know that these events did not occur at the hands of individuals who claimed to be Christians, but who in fact were crazed, sick, and misguided. They were, instead, actions of sincere church members living out the practical consequences of a theological exclusivism they learned in the church.[3]

Theologian Mark Heim puts the position of the majority of mainline Christians in perspective when he says that though this ugly side of church history ought to produce a humility among Christians that "shapes our encounter with other religions," at the same time the church's checkered past is not reason for giving up the Christian witness.[4] A humble church can be a repentant church that comes clean and admits that Christians have made exclusivistic claims, the consequences of which have been a marked contrast to the One in whose name these claims have been made.

At the same time, humility does not mean the church should throw the baby out with the bath water. The majority of mainline Christians still believe God was in Christ and that salvation was wrought in his life, death, and resurrection. They are not willing to give up their faith for the sake of what Heim calls "ice cream" pluralism, which treats differences of faith as if they are different flavors of ice cream.[5] Quite the opposite. Whether they can articulate it or not, they would affirm precisely the kind of genuine religious pluralism he describes when he writes:

> True pluralism...does not assume that all can be melted into the same basic substances. It leaves open the possibility that some faiths, at least, might be forms of the same thing. It does not rule this out, but it does not assume it either. Rather than supposing that real differences are dangerous, and ought to be diffused from the beginning, true pluralism will allow that we may differ even over issues of the greatest importance.[6]

No doubt many mainline Christians have never considered all the theological implications of religious pluralism or Christian exclusivism, but my experience has been that when pressed they have some sense that there are fundamental questions about how Christians relate to non-Christians that need to be addressed.[7] But they have not abandoned evangelism. What they have rejected is the kind of crass marketing of the gospel that passes for evangelism. I believe most mainliners would fully embrace the ministry of evangelism if they could see how it might function in the world they live in today.

This chapter seeks to offer precisely this. It argues for a theological foundation for evangelism that undergirds a ministry of evangelism that fits who mainliners are. This is not to suggest that a theology of evangelism in itself will save the day for mainline churches. But if the ministry of evangelism has any chance of being reclaimed by them, it will happen only as mainline theology guides evangelistic methodology.

Let me begin with a skeletal definition of evangelism that will be discussed at length in the next chapter. For our purposes here it will provide a reference point for the rest of the chapter. Simply put, evangelism is the ministry of *witnessing to Jesus Christ*. I suspect this does not strike anyone as either profound or provocative, but I hope by the end of the book the provocative dimension of witness evangelism will be evident. At any rate, I believe the biblical view of evangelism is that it is the ministry of individuals and churches witnessing to their own conversion, witnessing to their trust in and experience of the truth that God was in Christ reconciling the world to God's self (2 Corinthians 5:19).

With this in mind, I want to consider the Christian affirmation of salvation in Jesus Christ within the context of what I believe is the most basic claim of scripture, that God alone is sovereign, and that divine sovereignty is absolute.[8] This claim is rooted in the nature of God and is definitive for the divine/human relationship. To believe in the absoluteness of the sovereignty of God is to believe that in the end God always has the final word, that God initiates and humankind responds, and that this response in no way limits the divine initiative. A sovereign God is One who cares for creation—is even supremely related to it, to use Charles Hartshorne's phrase[9]—but is also free to act as God chooses. In short, the freedom of humankind is always and forever limited by the absoluteness of God's sovereignty. To unpack what this means in regard to the Christian belief in salvation in Jesus Christ, I want to focus on the confessional statement "Jesus is Lord and Savior."

In those traditions that practice believer's baptism, such as my own, the baptism of a new convert is preceded by the person answering the following question: "Do you believe that Jesus is the Christ, the Son of the Living God, and do you accept him as your (personal) Lord and Savior?" This action on the believer's part is called "making the Good Confession."

It is only after this act of confession that one is baptized. I think it is safe to say that, even among traditions that practice infant baptism, this confession is considered a statement of the basic claim of Christian theology, that Jesus Christ was—and is—the Son of God through whom God offers salvation from sin to all who believe in Jesus. But I want to suggest that in fact this statement reinforces the notion that God's saving action in Jesus Christ is dependent upon human response and thus creates an unacceptable limitation on divine sovereignty. More consistent with the absoluteness of God's sovereignty would be a reversal of this confession so that what we confess is "Jesus Christ as Savior and Lord." More than a harmless difference in semantics, to confess Jesus is "Savior and Lord," rather than Jesus is "Lord and Savior," is to address the issue of what it means for God to be God, and what it means for Christians to claim salvation in Jesus Christ. This is because to believe Jesus was Savior before he was Lord is to understand the gift of salvation in him as an act of a sovereign God. In other words, that God was in Christ reconciling the world to God's self was an act independent of human response. In fact, it was an act, as Paul also says, that occurred yet while we were sinners:

> For while we were still weak, at the right time Christ died for the ungodly. Indeed, rarely will anyone die for a righteous person—though perhaps for a good person someone might actually dare to die. But God proves his love for us in that while we still were sinners Christ died for us. (Romans 5:6–8)

Matthew's version of the Great Commission (see Chapter 6 for a more extended discussion of this text) makes the same point. Jesus says that all power in heaven and on earth has been given to him (Matthew 28:18). In this single sentence, Matthew declares that God's act of salvation in the crucifixion/resurrection event preceded the church's claim to his lordship, that as Savior Jesus has been given all authority in heaven and on earth before the church recognized him as Lord. This is a theological assertion that God's gift of grace precedes repentance, precedes faith, precedes making any "good confession." In short, Matthew 28:18 declares that God's gift of salvation in Jesus Christ precedes and is independent of human response. To confess Jesus is Savior and Lord means the church is acknowledging this central affirmation of scripture that God alone is sovereign. Further, it means acknowledging that God's actions are never dependent upon human response. A sovereign God is One who initiates rather than reacts, One who acts without the need for human consultation, and certainly without the need for human approval, either before or after the act. No one consciously declares, of course, that God is dependent on human response, but this is precisely what the traditional confession actually suggests. Confessing Jesus as Savior and Lord, on the other hand, acknowledges that God is free to act in whatever way God chooses, and that we believe God has chosen to give us the gift of salvation in Jesus. To put it succinctly, confessing first that Jesus is "Lord" implies that he is "Savior" only if he is Lord, when in truth the opposite is the case. We have the chance to call him "Lord" only because God chose to make him "Savior." It is not that our response is unimportant or unnecessary, only that it is just that, a response to what God has already done.

The reason the church persists in confessing Jesus as "Lord and Savior" is because we interpret "sin" as a moral problem and, therefore, something for which forgiveness is required before one can be saved. The effect of this understanding of sin is that it makes forgiveness dependent on the will of the offender in wanting it, asking for it, even begging for it, rather than on the act of God in Jesus Christ. Fundamentally "sin" is a theological problem that has existential consequences ("sins"). It is separation or alienation from God, a state of estrangement.[10] This condition is what God chose to forgive in the saving event of the crucifixion and resurrection of Jesus. Thus, God forgave "sin," estrangement from God, in Jesus Christ, "while we were yet sinners," as Paul said. "Sins," that is, acts that are considered sinful, are the expressions of "sin."[11] Human beings, Christians and non-Christian alike, have never been, and so far as we know, will never be, free from "sins" because of this basic alienation from God, for which we have been forgiven. This forgiveness is the basis for our hope. Because we do the very things we don't want to do, and don't do the things we want to do (Romans 7:15), there is no escaping the reality of sin. The good news which God has revealed in Jesus is the divine choice of forgiveness. We can interpret this choice to mean that God is gracious, giving us what we do not deserve, divine forgiveness and presence. Thus, salvation in Jesus Christ is the revelation of the unmerited gift of God's forgiveness and eternal presence.

The revelation of this gift is what makes life with God possible. Christians are those who trust Jesus as Lord because we believe that God made him Savior by raising him from the dead, forgiving our sins, and promising always to be in our future. Though we deserve to be rejected, God has shown us that we will never be forsaken or condemned. This is the merciful choice of the only true sovereign God. Were the divine/human relationship to depend upon our will or our ability to respond appropriately to God, the relationship would be doomed from the beginning. We choose death over life. The sins of the flesh are always with us. The spirit may be willing, but the flesh will always be weak. But God has chosen to be with us in spite of ourselves. That is why the story of Jesus is good news. He was Savior before the church ever called him Lord.

All that I have said is only to affirm the radical nature of divine grace that God made known in Jesus. Unfortunately, the church has tended toward "domesticating" grace by its failure to interpret the act of salvation in Jesus within the context of divine sovereignty. As a result it has persisted in making salvation conditional upon human response, i.e., confessing Jesus as Lord and Savior. To offset this message, which rejects the absoluteness of divine sovereignty, the church has appealed to the demands of divine justice. God must be satisfied. A payment for "sin" must be made. Human beings must be held accountable for their rejection of God's will. But if Jesus reveals anything to us about the nature of God, it is that while we deserve justice, that is, getting what we deserve, God has chosen to relate to us in grace, giving us what we don't deserve.

As the implications of the radical nature of grace become apparent, then it also becomes clear that grace is an expression of the sovereignty of God. Salvation is possible because God is sovereign. Affirming faith in divine sovereignty is to take the risk of trusting ourselves to the absolute freedom of God to do whatever God chooses to do. If there are limitations on God, they are self-imposed. At the same time, the absoluteness of God's freedom ultimately places limits on human freedom.[12] While it is true that we are free to choose not to acknowledge God's sovereignty, it is just as true to say that we are not free to limit it. This is the primary difference between divine and human freedom. God limits the ultimate effects of human freedom; we do not limit the ultimate effects of God's sovereignty.

The absoluteness of God's sovereignty is clearly a radical concept, as Jesus' parable of the laborers in the vineyard illustrates (Matthew 20:1–16). The owner of the vineyard hires laborers at different times of the day. Even though some of them work more hours than others, the owner pays them all the same wage for the day's work. As one might expect, those who work all day become angry with the owner because he does not pay them more than the others. The owner's reply to their complaint is the key to the parable's word about God's sovereignty:

> Take what belongs to you, and go; I choose to give to this last the same as I give to you. Am I not allowed to do what I choose with what belongs to me? Or are you envious because I am generous?
>
> (Matthew 20:14–15)

The laborers resisted the freedom of the owner to do what he wanted with what belonged to him. If, as verse 1 says, this is a parable about the reign of God, then the owner's actions reveal the actions of God. God is free to do what God wants with what belongs to God, which is the whole of creation. That is the nature of God's sovereignty.

The subject of divine sovereignty is found throughout scripture. Man and woman confront divine sovereignty in the garden (Genesis 2:4—3:24). The fruit of the tree from which they were forbidden to eat symbolizes ultimate knowledge.[13] It was the tree of the knowledge of good and evil (2:17). According to the story, to have knowledge of good and evil means to possess ultimate knowledge. But such knowledge belongs only to God. We know evil and good exist. We do not know their origins or purpose. Thus, the garden story is about humankind's resistance to our role as creatures and to God as the only sovereign One. Yet even when man and woman eat the apple, an act in defiance of divine sovereignty, God, in God's sovereignty, chooses to respond graciously. The man and woman do not receive justice. They had been told that if they ate of the forbidden fruit they would surely die (2:17). But instead, even though they are banished from the garden to make it on their own, they are allowed to live (3:23–24). Death is postponed. Yet the ultimate irony in the story is that humankind does gain at least partial knowledge of good and evil (3:22). The banishment serves to preserve the integrity of divine sovereignty when it declares that full knowledge of creation resides only with God. Human access to the mystery of life and death is limited, as if we were seeing in a mirror dimly (1 Corinthians 13:12).

The story of the flood (Genesis 7—8) is another example of the affirmation of God's sovereignty. Humankind deserves to die; thus, the flood becomes an act of redemption in that humankind is spared (grace) when death is warranted (justice). It is a story of God re-creating life. In the story of the Tower of Babel (Genesis 11:1–9), humankind seeks to make a name for themselves, which means they seek to hold power equal to God's. But God, as the One who is truly sovereign, confounds them by creating language barriers. The first commandment is: "You shall have no other gods before me" (Exodus 20:2–3). Further, quoting the Shema (Deuteronomy 6:4), Jesus says, "You shall love the LORD your God with all your heart, and with all your soul, and with all your mind. This is the greatest and first commandment" (Matthew 22:37–38).

It is possible that the difference between the true and false prophets in Israel turned on this same issue. On the face of it, reliable predictions of the future seemed to be what distinguished them. In his debate with the prophet Hananiah, Jeremiah at one point declares as much: "As for the prophet who prophesies peace, when the word of that prophet comes true, then it will be known that the LORD has truly sent the prophet" (Jeremiah 28:9). The problem, of course, was that this required the people to wait for the future to reveal who was telling the truth and who was not. But what were they to do in the meantime? Perhaps the debate between Hananiah and Jeremiah provides some guidance (Jeremiah 28). The issue was what would happen now that King Nebuchadnezzar of Babylon had taken the royal family of Judah into exile. Hananiah predicts God will return them within two years and Israel will prosper once again. Jeremiah responds with the hope that Hananiah has spoken the truth but proceeds to declare that no such return will occur. The basis of their disagreement may be the basis for distinguishing true and false prophets in every generation. Hananiah's prediction rested on his conviction that God was the God of Israel. Thus, God would act always to protect the covenant nation. Jeremiah, on the other hand, proclaims the absolute sovereignty of God and declares that God is free to choose not to bring the royal family home, and that in fact God will make Israel serve Nebuchadnezzar:

> Sometime after the prophet Hananiah had broken the yoke from the neck of the prophet Jeremiah, the word

of the LORD came to Jeremiah: Go, tell Hananiah, Thus says the LORD: You have broken wooden bars only to forge iron bars in place of them! For thus says the LORD of hosts, the God of Israel: I have put an iron yoke on the neck of all these nations so that they may serve King Nebuchadnezzar of Babylon, and they shall indeed serve him; I have even given him the wild animals. (28:12–14)

Then Jeremiah speaks directly to Hananiah:

Listen, Hananiah, the LORD has not sent you, and you made this people trust in a lie. Therefore thus says the LORD: I am going to send you off the face of the earth. Within this year you will be dead, because you have spoken rebellion against the LORD. In that same year, in the seventh month, the prophet Hananiah died. (28:15–17)

This reading of the debate between Hananiah and Jeremiah suggests that the truth or falsity of the prophet's words depended on which one understood the freedom of God's sovereignty and which one tried to place limitations on it.[14]

We can see, then, that the focus of the parable of the laborers in the vineyard is consistent with the theme of the absolute sovereignty of God throughout the Bible. Understanding salvation in Jesus Christ within the context of divine sovereignty releases the church from a presumption about and preoccupation with who is and is not among the redeemed of God. We leave that to God, trusting that the grace revealed in Jesus Christ extends to whomever God chooses. Moreover, we believe not only the church, but all the world lives under this mercy.

But the freedom of divine sovereignty is not something about which the community of God's people, whether Jewish or Christian, has ever been fully comfortable and, thus, fully embraced. Sovereignty has the look of being unfair, even unjust. For a church preoccupied with who is "in" and who is "not in" regarding the kingdom of God, we engage in theological irony in that we who covet absoluteness with human freedom desire to place limits on the freedom of God. In the process we resist accepting that we are not coequals with God in the created order, that the vineyard, i.e., the world, belongs to God, not to us, and that our role is the same as the workers in the vineyard. Even if we become stewards of the vineyard, or creation (Genesis 2:19), that does not change the fact that God alone is sovereign.

Is Jesus the Only Way?

This question is the ultimate issue in Christian exclusivism. If Jesus is the only way, then all other questions have been answered. The evangelistic imperative is clear. Only the church has the message of salvation. Concern for religious pluralism is misplaced. Christians simply need to get into the world and convert all non-Christians to Christ. Certainly those in the church who are on the theological right, most of whom are proponents of the church growth movement, would answer the question this way. That is because they are at home with making judgments about who is "in" and who is "out" in the reign of God. Peter Wagner, the most dominant voice in the church growth movement today, describes this kind of Christian exclusivism as what he calls "non-negotiable" theological assumptions of church growth evangelism.[15] They are:

1. The glory of God as the chief end of humans
2. The lordship of Jesus Christ
3. The normative authority of the scripture (meaning "infallible")
4. The ultimate eschatological reality of sin, salvation, and eternal life (salvation belongs only to Christians)[16]
5. The personal ministry of the Holy Spirit

Mainline Christians can certainly affirm these assumptions, but not uncritically. For example, we accept the notion that the chief aim of humankind is to glorify God and God only, as the Westminister Confession states. We also affirm the lordship of Jesus Christ, as well as the personal ministry of the Holy Spirit. We can even affirm the third assumption that the authority of scripture is normative in the church. But the doctrine of the "infallibility" of scripture Wagner attaches to it poses a serious problem. The fact is, the Bible's being normative does not require assent to scriptural infallibility, as Wagner suggests. Indeed, the whole issue of infallibility is bogus. At the very least it would take an infallible mind to discern the truth of an infallible text. And if what was infallible was the original text, as is often argued, that, too, has no practical consequence, since no original texts are extant, only copies, and then more fragments than whole manuscripts. Further, to tie inspiration to infallibility is simply to misunderstand what the inspiration of scripture actually means.[17]

But Wagner does this precisely because of assumption number four, which states Christian exclusivism rather bluntly: Salvation belongs only to Christians. Wagner argues that this is the inevitable conclusion of the Christian claim that salvation is in Jesus Christ. For mainline Christians, however, there is another perspective that allows us to affirm faith in Jesus Christ as "Savior and Lord" without this kind of judgmentalism that presumes the right to draw circles around divine love, a judgmentalism that Heim calls "imperial particularity."[18]

Two primary biblical texts undergird the argument that the only "Bible-based" answer to the question "Is Jesus the only Savior?" is "Yes." One contains the words of Jesus himself found in John 14:6, "I am the way, and the truth, and the life. No one comes to the Father except through me." The other are the words of the apostle Peter in Acts 4:12, where he declares, "There is salvation in no one else, for there is no other name under heaven given among mortals by which we must be saved." Quite simply, the argument goes, these two texts make the case for Christian exclusivism. But I suggest that this appeal to John 14:6 and Acts 4:12 is a bit too facile. Actually, a careful and honest look at both texts makes it rather obvious that such exclusivism is actually imposed on them. Neither even considers the issue of whether or not Jesus is the only Savior. Let us look at both, beginning with the Acts passage, since it was written before the Gospel of John.

Scholars have not found it easy to date the writing of Acts, but it is generally thought to have been written between 64 and 85 C.E. Any date within this time frame would reflect a time in the church when the controversy between Jewish Christians, Gentile Christians, and Jews was growing in intensity, resulting in a complete schism between synagogue and church by 130 C.E.[19] Luke describes the church's beginnings with the final appearance of Jesus to the disciples with instruction that they are to wait in Jerusalem until they receive the power of the Holy Spirit, and only then begin witnessing to him (Acts 1:8). The Spirit descends upon them at Pentecost, which sets the stage for the sermon Peter preaches to the Jews gathered for the festival. John also begins to preach openly about Jesus, and he and Peter are arrested and brought before the Sanhedrin Council to defend themselves (4:1–12). It is before these priests that Peter makes the statement with which we are concerned.

This in itself is significant for understanding this passage. It is widely thought that the Sanhedrin was a group of priests whose purpose was to guide the religious life of the Jews. But New Testament scholar Howard Clark Kee says this type of Sanhedrin came to life much later. What existed at the time of Jesus was the *synedrion*, a council appointed by Roman authorities whose members were a select group of Jewish leaders who had agreed to cooperate for the purpose of maintaining Roman power.[20] This being the case, Peter's words were obviously directed at priests who were compromising faith in the God of Israel, who had promised an Anointed One who was of the seed of Abraham (Genesis 12:3). Peter believed Jesus was the one for whom they had been waiting. The Council's sole concern was not whether this was true, but to prevent the followers of Jesus from stirring up trouble with the Romans. In a real sense Peter was testifying to what he believed was the continuing vitality of the Jewish people and their faith in God as one who is merciful.

This suggests another important factor, that there is no evidence that Peter understood Jesus apart from Judaism. According to Acts itself, the conversion of the apostle Paul was still a future event at this time, so at this juncture in the story the mission to the Gentiles had not begun. When it did, Paul says Peter waffled on the issue of Gentiles being required to become Jews in order to be Christians. He says Peter first agreed with Paul that Torah was not binding on Gentiles but later reversed himself under pressure from Jerusalem leaders (Galatians 2:11–14). This means that on the face of it the text is saying that Peter's defense was a debate among Jews about Judaism. Any interpretation that he is arguing for the supremacy of Christ over Judaism is simply an interpolation. The split between the synagogue and church that occurred later was not even in the wind at this point. No church existed, nor even any expectation of one. Christians were Jews who followed Jesus. Thus, Peter was arguing for Jesus' being the Messiah of Judaism whom the religious leaders had rejected. He believed Jesus was raised from the dead and that this event should be sufficient evidence of Jesus' messiahship (4:10–11) and, thus, the fulfillment of Jewish hopes.

To argue, therefore, that this text supports the church's claim of the supremacy of Christianity is to read back into the text that which the text itself does not say, and could not say, given the historical situation. It is, of course, likely that Luke was using Peter's defense to set the stage for the Gentile mission he spends most of Acts describing. But again, if Luke's audience was Jewish Christians, as is most probable, then he was simply reassuring them with the words of Peter that they were being faithful Jews in following Jesus. If his audience was Gentile Christians, then he was reassuring them that there is no other name, save the name of Jesus, whereby they could be saved. In other words, as Paul's preaching proclaimed, Torah is not binding on Gentiles. This is obviously still true today. For Christians, there is no other name under heaven given among mortals by which we are saved except the name of Jesus. But saying this is not the same thing as saying that all non-Christians are condemned to hell. To say that is to claim knowledge that belongs only to God. Our task is simply to tell the truth we know for ourselves. That is the theological foundation for evangelism that acknowledges God alone is sovereign.

The John text (14:6) presents us with words attributed to Jesus himself that speak of the intimate relationship that existed between Jesus and God.[21] To know Jesus is to know God, a theme also found in Matthew and Luke (Matthew 11:27, Luke 10:22). The text focuses on Jesus' being "the Way" to God, a concept with a long history "originating in the Old Testament, modified by sectarian Jewish thought illustrated at Qumran [Dead Sea Scrolls], and finally adopted by the Christian community as a self-designation."[22] Not only is Jesus the Way, he is also the Truth and the Life. All three designations declare that Jesus is the sure road to God. To receive him is to receive the One who sent him, which John says is the reason why he wrote his Gospel: "But these are written so that you may come to believe that Jesus is the Messiah, the Son of God, and that through believing you may have life in his name" (20:31).

Is this the same thing as saying Jesus is the "only" way to God? If we again try to understand the text within its historical setting, then it is a text reflecting the Christian struggle for legitimacy in its conflict with Judaism. John's Gospel was written near the time of the final split between synagogue and church, most probably between 90 and 100 C.E.[23] Not unlike Peter's sermon in Acts, the Gospel offers assurance that Jesus is the Messiah, and that anyone willing to believe that will experience "life" in his name. If John is writing to Jewish Christians who were continuing their observance of Torah law, he is offering them encouragement to keep the faith against pressures not to. If he is writing to Gentile Christians, then he is making the same case that Paul makes in Galatians, that for Gentiles for whom Torah law is not binding, Jesus is the Way, the Truth, and the Life they can count on to connect them to God. There is no need to add the law to their faith. Jesus is sufficient for salvation. More probable, however, is that John was writing to Christian believers, Jewish or Gentile, for the purpose of rooting them deeper in their faith.[24] Moreover, the purpose of the Gospel stated in 20:31 should not be interpreted as primarily missionary, but as a way of augmenting the faith believers already have.[25] Thus, as we saw in Acts 4, to claim John 14:6 declares Jesus is the only Savior is at the very least pushing the text to say more than it actually says.

Actually, though, I think John's stated purpose for his Gospel in 20:31 points to the fact that forcing 14:6 into an unnecessary Christian exclusivism is not only unwarranted, but unnecessary. While Christians believe there is "objective" truth in God's grace being revealed in Jesus Christ, it is also true that the content of all Christian claims ultimately has to be borne out in the life of the hearer. The church today can say that Jesus is the Way, the Truth, and the Life not solely because John recorded these words, but because the truth of these words is confirmed by the relationship with Jesus believers have experienced, as John said they would.[26] Christians do not simply have life. We have life in Jesus Christ. And because we do, we have life with God. This is the truth to which the church is called to witness.

This brief analysis of Acts 4:11 and John 14:6 may not satisfy Christians determined to practice persuasive evangelism in which they count themselves among the "saved" and those to whom they go as the "lost." Minimally, however, I think it has been shown that there is more than one way to interpret these verses, and that no single

interpretation can make an absolute claim without violating
the texts themselves. Further, the nature of the Christian
gospel in no way suggests that the validity of Christianity
depends upon the invalidity of all other religions because
that is not where the matter turns. At issue is whether
Christians can trust that Jesus Christ reveals the truth about
a God who is both gracious and sovereign. Both of the texts
we have discussed answer this question with a resounding
Yes, offering mainline churches a theological basis for the
ministry of evangelism by declaring without hesitation that
as Christians we know one Way to God. That Way is Jesus
Christ.[27]

The Judgment of God

But even if it is acknowledged that the above texts provide
an unreliable justification for the belief in salvation for
Christians only, the issue is not yet settled. The question of
the church's teaching about divine judgment has yet to be
discussed and cannot be ignored. If it is possible that non-
Christians might be included in God's covenant of salvation,
then what meaning, or even appropriateness, does the
church's teaching about heaven and hell any longer hold?
Essentially the sticking point is the fact that a non-judgmental
theology for evangelism is understood as a de facto basis for
universal salvation. I want to show why this is not the case.

It goes without saying that the church has played the
judgment card for most of its history, hoping that fear would
be a motivator for repentance and conversion. The "hell fire
and damnation" sermons heard from pulpits through the
centuries have used fear in this way. Preaching was
understood as the opportunity to persuade recalcitrant
sinners to make a turn before it was too late. In essence, fear
and persuasion became constitutive of the church's
evangelistic appeal. Not only is neither necessary, but both
are ineffective. On the contrary, a nonjudgmental theology
points us in another direction, where gratitude is the

motivator for repentance, and attraction is evangelism's most effective methodology.

Keep in mind that the critical factor in thinking about divine judgment is what we have been pointing to throughout this chapter, the absolute sovereignty of God. Understood in this context, God's judgment can be affirmed in two manifestations. The first is what can be called the *ultimate* judgment of God. Ultimate judgment has to do with "sin." At its most extreme point, it means the end of life, the final and irredeemable chapter, a death from which there is no escape. This kind of judgment is irrevocable. Once passed, it is finished. Ironically, The Revelation to John, usually interpreted as a statement assuring hell for nonbelievers, actually refers to ultimate judgment in what it calls "the second death":

> Then Death and Hades were thrown into the lake of fire. This is the second death, the lake of fire.…But as for the cowardly, the faithless, the polluted, the murderers, the fornicators, the sorcerers, the idolaters, and all liars, their place will be in the lake that burns with fire and sulfur, which is the second death. (20:14; 21:8)

Further, Revelation makes it clear that it is not given to human beings to know how "second death" will be determined, only that in the freedom of divine sovereignty, God can do what God wills to do. We have no knowledge other than this, though the church has made claims to the contrary for centuries. From the perspective of Matthew's Gospel, the main thing Jesus said about it is that it will be based upon unexpected criteria and the very people who think they know who will be "in" and who will be "out" will be the most surprised of all: "Then the righteous will answer him, 'Lord, when was it that we saw you…?'" (Matthew 25:37). Perhaps all the church needs to know about ultimate judgment is that the sovereignty of God underscores the fact that it is best left to God in the hope and trust that divine grace will be God's ultimate judgment.

A second judgment is what I call *existential* judgment. This is the type of judgment the apostle Paul was talking about when he wrote, "Do not be deceived; God is not mocked, for you reap whatever you sow" (Galatians 6:7). Existential judgment is God allowing humankind the freedom to make choices. We can serve or not serve God. But freedom carries with it both the joy of good decisions and the consequences of bad ones. Theologically, this means we bear responsibility for moral/ethical decisions. Further, it means God respects human freedom to the point of there being no escape from the effects of "sins." We love and hate, act responsibly and irresponsibly, make peace and war, honor commitments and turn our backs on them, perform selfless and selfish deeds with their commensurate consequences, positive and negative. Human freedom even means we sometimes bear the consequences of other people's decisions, good and bad alike. Thus, because of God's choice to respect human freedom, we live in the face of existential judgment every day. As Paul says, we reap what we sow, good or bad.

Existential judgment was at work in the crucifixion of Jesus. In their freedom, a freedom God chose not to nullify, human beings put Jesus to death. In the context of divine sovereignty, God chose to work within the circumstances this act created. The resurrection becomes God's answer as the sovereign One to human freedom. God will be with us even though we reject God. Further, the resurrection hints at the hope we have in facing God's ultimate judgment. Jesus' death and resurrection tell us that we can trust that God will forever act out of grace rather than justice. Justice would require condemnation, but in Jesus, God has chosen forgiveness instead. This means that death does not have the final word. Life does. God raised Jesus and made him the first fruits of those who have died (1 Corinthians 15:20). This is not what we deserved. We are recipients of the unmerited choice of God to make covenant with us, an act of a sovereign God who has chosen to love us in spite of ourselves. This is the heart of the Christian gospel. We believe that God has shown us all we need to know in Jesus Christ. Our relationship with him is the key to our existence. Beyond this nothing more is needed. How God acts outside of the center of Christian experience is best left to God, an acceptance of the limits of human knowledge man and woman first encountered in the Garden. We live and die in the face of the mystery as we trust the one who alone is sovereign.

To deny this reality is to tribalize God. The gospel of Jesus Christ declares that we belong to God. God does not belong to us. It is a message people have not found easy to hear. Luke tells us that when Jesus spoke it in his hometown synagogue, the people were filled with rage (4:28). All he had said was that God sent Elijah to give food to a widow at Zarephath during a famine in Israel, and sent Elisha to heal Naaman, the captain of the Syrian army, of leprosy when there were many lepers in Israel. Blinded by tribalization, the people were angered by the sovereignty of God. It was not enough that they belonged to God. They wanted God to belong to them. Part of the truth of our salvation is that the God of Jesus Christ is sovereign. We are called to follow Jesus. We cannot own God.[28]

Understanding Jesus within the context of divine sovereignty means in the deepest sense that our salvation does not depend upon what is in our hearts, but what is in the heart of God. At the same time, discipleship as a response to this gift does not depend upon what is in the heart of God, but what is in ours. If salvation is an act of a sovereign God, discipleship is an act of human freedom. It is the human response to the gift of God's salvation in which we commit ourselves to a lifetime of gratitude. It is a response that begins in repentance, wherein we confront the ugliness of our idolatrous ways and confess our need for forgiveness.

This is the power of gratitude. A grateful people and a grateful church desire to witness to love and grace that exceed the human reach of understanding. The church witnesses to the gift of life we are free to live under God's mercy, not out of fear but out of gratitude. Gratitude has the power to inspire one to commit one's whole life to serve God because it is rooted in the good news that, in spite of sin, we are accepted by God.[29] Taking issue with the widely-held belief that the "command" of the Great Commission was the motivation for evangelism in the early church, Michael Green says that loving gratitude was the main motive for the evangelistic witness of the early church, gratitude that arose from experiencing being loved by God in Jesus Christ: "This gratitude, devotion, dedication to the Lord who had rescued them and given them a new life…was the main motive in evangelism in the early church."[30] This same gratitude has the power today to lead the church into the kind of commitment that is willing to make any sacrifice for the sake of the gospel.

Unfortunately, the church has often failed to live out of a sense of gratitude because it has been reluctant to trust in the power of divine love to attract. It now must reclaim its faith in the winsomeness of divine love. Indeed, if evangelism has a strategy, it is the strategy of attraction, not promotion, and certainly not promotion of itself. Rather than focusing on witnessing to its belief in and experience of this love, the church has chosen to preach a gospel of conditional salvation, trying feverishly to persuade people to accept Jesus in order to be saved. This is a failure to understand that when discipleship arises from anything other than gratitude, grace is compromised. Witness evangelism does call people to discipleship, not so they might be saved, but so they might learn how to celebrate and witness to the gift of salvation they have been given in Jesus Christ. It declares that nothing can be done to deserve this gift, not even a confession of faith. Earning God's love is not possible. Being grateful for it and celebrating it is.

Is this "cheap grace"?[31] If salvation is independent of human response, then why not live any way we want to live? Why not be a taker rather than a giver? Let the survival of the fittest rule the world. Apparently this was the first objection the apostle Paul encountered when he described what God had done in Christ as a gracious gift: "Should we continue in sin in order that grace may abound?" Paul asked (Romans 6:1). "By no means," he answered (6:2). What did he mean? Precisely that human freedom under the sovereignty of God leads to responsibility. One does not do anything one chooses because of grace. Rather, when grace is truly experienced, one seeks to please the Giver of grace all the more. One who would live irresponsibly because of grace will live irresponsibly anyway. Making grace conditional is not an answer to the irresponsible use of freedom. Using freedom for a license to do anything we want to do is a clear sign that we have never encountered God's grace in the first place. One who has never encountered God's grace does not possess, or is not possessed by, gratitude. But one who has had this encounter cannot *not* be possessed by gratitude. And within the limitations of being human, one who is possessed by gratitude of necessity takes the responsibility of freedom seriously—not flawlessly, but seriously.

From this perspective, then, discipleship is the celebration of grace. It is living a joyous life under the love and mercy of God revealed in Jesus Christ. Jean Vanier says that a community truly connected to Jesus is a community that learns how to celebrate. He does not mean by this the kind of artificial celebration the world knows about. Rather, Vanier says Christian celebration means

> to share what and who we truly are; it is to express our love for one another, our hopes, and to rejoice in being together as parts of the same body. As we go from singing, dance, and laughter into silence, there will be a sense of presence. Somewhere at the heart of celebration there is the consciousness of the presence of Jesus Christ. Christ is the one who is our cornerstone, the one who has drawn us together, and we rejoice because he is present with us.

Further, he calls Christian celebration "eucharist."

Eucharist is community celebration—and I do not mean here just the eucharistic worship…but also the deep silence in communion, one with another and with Christ.…Celebration is not just going to eucharistic worship together. Celebration is being a eucharistic people who sing their thanks because they have been called together as one people in order to bring life to others.[32]

Thus, we have come full circle. The Christian witness in the world is rooted in the church being a eucharistic community. This ministry of evangelism is the way we show God gratitude for the gift of salvation in Jesus Christ, who is the One we trust and have experienced as the Way, the Truth, and the Life. It matters not if there is another way to encounter this truth we know in Jesus. We tell our story, his story, in the hope and anticipation that the Spirit will bring others both to believe and experience its truth. That is what the ministry of evangelism is, witnessing to that which we know through faith and experience. It is a description of this ministry to which we now turn our attention.

NOTES

[1] See Darrell L. Guder's article in which he argues that the church growth movement resists the kind of theological reflection I am talking about and instead concerns itself primarily with methodologies. "Evangelism and the Debate over Church Growth," *Interpretation*, 48:2, April, 1994, p. 147.

[2] Thomas C. Oden, *After Modernity, What?* (Grand Rapids: Zondervan, 1990). See especially chapters 7–8, in which Oden names the negative effects of higher critical study and the reasons its continued use has a place in the church. Building on but going beyond other critical methods, see also the work of James A. Sanders and Brevard Childs, whose canonical critical approach to scripture attempts to put the Bible back together.

[3] Martin Luther, for example, called for the expulsion from Germany of all unconverted Jews in the last sermon he ever preached.

[4] S. Mark Heim, *Is Christ the Only Way?* (Valley Forge: Judson Press, 1985), p. 20.

[5] Ibid., p. 30.

[6] Ibid. Heim expands this discussion of "true" religious pluralism in his book *Salvations: Truth and Difference in Religion* (New York: Orbis Books, 1995), in which he argues that one's own faith is strengthened both in knowing other traditions and in recognizing the real differences that exist between traditions.

[7] To explore in depth some of the work being done on a post-Holocaust Christian theology, see the works of Paul Van Buren (*The Jewish Christian Reality*, 3 vols., New York: Seabury, 1980, 1983, 1988) and Clark M. Williamson (*A Guest in the House of Israel*, Louisville: Westminster John Knox, 1993).

[8] J. I. Packer seeks to recover this central belief for evangelism *(Evangelism and the Sovereignty of God*, Downers Grove: InterVarsity Press, 1961). Lesslie Newbigin also emphasizes the sovereignty of God, but in my estimation doing so within the concept of divine election diminishes the impact of his argument *(The Open Secret*, Grand Rapids: Eerdmans, 1978, pp. 73–86). I also think Heim misses the mark when he says that "Christ is God's self-characterization" (*Is Christ the Only Way?* p. 143 [See note 4, ch. 2]), but fails to mention that central to this "self-characterization" is divine sovereignty. This omission leaves his position vulnerable to being interpreted as a subtle form of Christian exclusivism because it has no element that transcends Christianity and mitigates replacing God with Christ, a danger Heim himself warns against.

[9] Charles Hartshorne, *The Divine Relativity* (New Haven: Yale University Press, 1964).

[10] By "estrangement" I mean *hubris*, as Tillich defined it, rather than unbelief: "*Hubris* is the self-elevation of man into the sphere of the divine." Paul Tillich, *Systematic Theology: Three Volumes in One* (Chicago: The University of Chicago Press, 1967), Vol. 2, p. 50.

[11] Ibid., p. 46.

[12] Tillich characterizes human freedom as always finite because "all potentialities which constitute [human] freedom are limited by the opposite pole, [human] destiny" (ibid., p. 32). I am, on the other hand, speaking of human freedom in existential terms in the sense of the effect of God's nature on human existence and the divine/human relationship.

[13] *Hubris*, see note 2.

[14] Based upon a lecture I heard by James A. Sanders in which he argued that this was the basis for the dispute between the prophets Hananiah and Jeremiah (Jeremiah 28).

[15] Peter Wagner, *Church Growth and the Whole Gospel: A Biblical Mandate* (San Francisco: Harper & Row, 1981), p. xiii. He expands these five non-negotiable assumptions to seven in his book, *Strategies for Church Growth* (Ventura, California: Regal, 1987), pp. 39–40. No doubt Wagner has been influenced by the Frankfurt Declaration of 1970, which also contained "seven indispensable basic elements of mission" that drew lines in the sand in much the same way. (See David Bosch, *Witness to the World*, Atlanta: John Knox Press, 1980, pp. 193–194.)

[16] Wagner states forthrightly that salvation is exclusively Christian in the expanded version of these assumptions in *Strategies for Church Growth*, previously mentioned.

[17] Inspiration is the belief that the Holy Spirit was at work in the lives of the biblical writers, making the Bible a reliable source for divine truth. Infallibility goes further and asserts that the Bible as the literal Word of God is incapable of being in error and, thus, the only source of normative religious teaching. It is, I believe, a bogus issue. Its validity requires one to disregard the higher critical study of scripture in regard to the history and development of the New Testament and the canon as a whole. Moreover, that no original manuscripts now exist, that no language can be translated word for word into another, and that it would require an infallible mind to understand or even recognize an infallible text in the first place, all make the issue of infallibility a non-issue. The inspiration of scripture is the only affirmation mainline Christians need to make.

[18] *Is Christ the Only Way?*, p. 125. (See note 4. ch. 2.)

[19] The primary focus of the synagogue/church controversy was whether Torah was binding on Gentile Christians. The apostle Paul won the argument he advanced in Galatians that it should not be, and by the first third of the second century the schism was completed.

[20] Howard Clark Kee, "What is the Meaning of 'The Jews' in the New Testament," *Explorations*, 11:1, 1997.

[21] The historicity of the words of Jesus found in the Gospels has been a point of regular debate among scholars. I have chosen to try to understand these texts as part of the church's canon. At the same time, though, I think it is shortsighted to dismiss the provocative work of the Jesus Seminar regarding the historical Jesus as a pursuit that stems from an erroneous view of the nature of the church's faith. In many respects the Seminar is seeking to bring into the church the studies of Jesus, scripture, and the canonical process that have for too long been confined to the academy. See especially Robert Funk's *Honest to Jesus* (San Francisco: HarperSan Francisco, 1996). Funk is the founder of the Seminar.

[22] Raymond E. Brown, *The Gospel of John, Vol. 2*, The Anchor Bible (New York: Doubleday, 1966), p. 628.

[23] Raymond E. Brown, *The Gospel of John*, Vol.1, The Anchor Bible (New York: Doubleday, 1966), p. LXXXIII.

[24] Ibid., p. LXXVIII.

[25] Ibid.

[26] If we ask the canonical critical question "How did John's Gospel get in the canon?" this is the answer. The formation of the canon was confirmation that the church had already experienced certain books as sacred texts. See James A. Sanders, *From Sacred Story to Sacred Texts: Canon as Paradigm* (Philadelphia: Fortress, 1987).

[27] The fact that Christians do not simply accept the validity of other religions at face value stems from the fact that we can never affirm any claim that contradicts the gospel's witness to divine grace as it is revealed in Jesus. Thus, religious pluralism calls on the church to be both open and cautious in assessing non-Christian beliefs.

[28] Heim puts it this way: "To say that God is decisively defined by Christ does not mean that God is *exhausted* in Christ or totally confined to Christ." *Is Christ the Only Way?*, p. 132. (See note 4, ch. 2.)

[29] Tillich described the encounter with divine grace this way in a sermon entitled "You Are Accepted" (*The Shaking of the Foundations*, New York: Scribner's Sons, 1948), p. 162.

[30] Michael Green, *Evangelism in the Early Church* (Grand Rapids: Eerdmans, 1970), p. 242.

[31] Bonhoeffer's call for costly discipleship does not abrogate salvation by grace. The issue is not whether we are faithful, i.e., follow the teachings of Jesus, but the *motivation* for discipleship. See Dietrich Bonhoeffer, *The Cost of Discipleship* (New York: MacMillan, 1959).

[32] Jean Vanier, *From Brokenness to Community* (New York: Paulist Press, 1992), p. 46.

3

Evangelism as Intentional Witnessing

T he American church of today finds itself in a culture not devoid of religious values, but one in which the need for meaning and belonging go largely unfulfilled. This is a situation made for a ministry of evangelism. But effectiveness in this ministry begins with a clear understanding of what it is. I believe the specific form of evangelism that fits the life of mainline churches is intentional witnessing. The key word is *intentional*.

The church speaks often about witnessing, but the talk usually lacks both intentionality and specificity. Witnessing doesn't just happen. It is a conscious decision and desire to name the name of Jesus as the One to whom one belongs. At times witnessing happens unexpectedly, quietly, without immediate notice. A word is spoken, and later we discover it played a decisive role in the spiritual growth of another. Even then that word is deeply rooted in the conscious choice to be connected to Jesus Christ. But intentional witnessing is the claim Jesus makes on his disciples. This is the heart of the ministry of evangelism. Being intentional means not being content just to let witness happen. It is seeking to acknowledge publicly that we are Christian, and that is why we are who we are and do what we do.

This intentionality in witnessing is what mainline churches have been neglecting. To some extent we have let it slip away or slowly erode. Perhaps to a greater extent we have overreacted to the kind of "Are you saved?" witnessing by fundamentalists that is intrusive and offensive. But offensive and arrogant evangelistic tactics are no excuse for giving up intentional witnessing. Actually, they make a more determined effort to be a winsome witness that is much more essential. But mainline churches have not risen to the challenge. We talk of letting our actions speak for us, as if the unchurched have some natural instinct for understanding our motivations and seeing the face of Christ in our deeds. Perhaps some do, but do not want to make the commitment to which discipleship calls them. Statistics, on the other hand, suggest that many more do not. Numbers do not tell us how many people have truly committed themselves to following Jesus, but they do provide some sense of who is attracted to our message and who is not. The facts are not encouraging. In 1985 nearly 40 percent of unchurched people surveyed said they would definitely attend church if invited by a family member or friend. By 1994 that figure had dropped to 20 percent.[1]

Intentional witness evangelism refuses to choose between actions and words. It refuses to accept the notion that speaking the name of Jesus while reaching out to another is inherently offensive, intrusive, or self-serving. It takes a "both-and" approach to evangelism. Common sense, discernment of *kairos* moments, and honoring personal and collective social and civil boundaries do not diminish intentional witnessing. If anything, they lend credibility to it. Unchurched people are not attracted to the Christian message when the messenger gets in the way. They will not respond positively to prescriptive judgmentalism. But they do respect the courage of convictions.

The church that speaks openly about God can trust that the Spirit will use that witness to convert. But the language of faith is the key. Mainline churches can no longer simply invite people to join the church and expect anything to change. We must invite people into the ranks of genuine discipleship. Diverse definitions of what that means may exist, but the ministry of evangelism requires that a church be very clear about how it understands Christian commitment, and that it is to this commitment that it witnesses. Unchurched people care little about the language of the church. If the language of faith makes sense to them, they will care enough about what is going on inside the church to come in to find out.

But what we are talking about goes much deeper than a conscious speaking of the name of the One who calls us to serve others. It means that every ministry, every action, every worship service, every meeting, every visible expression of the church, intentionally seeks to be a loving and attractive witness to the power of the gospel to give meaning and purpose to one's life. The most obvious ways to make a Christian witness are through the ministries in which a church engages. Evangelism is not a committee assignment. It isn't learning some special technique about how to lead a person to Christ. Evangelism is the conscious work of praising and revealing the name of Jesus in every action, word, and moment of the church's life.

Individuals have a role to play in this witness, but in the fullest sense evangelism is the ministry of the whole church at all times and in all places. In practical terms this means every aspect of a church's life must be permeated with the desire to witness. Choir members, church school teachers, committee members, governing board members, trustees, clerical and ministerial staff, everyone in the church must be conscious of the fact that what they do is all about naming the name of Jesus with integrity and attractiveness. Every decision is a witnessing decision. It is not about maintaining the institution. It is about being the body of Christ. It is not about making the organization run smoothly. It is about being a healthy member of an organism.

This brings us to the crux of the issue. Intentional witness evangelism cannot exist without being an expression of a deep and abiding connectedness to Jesus Christ. That is why I suggested in the Introduction that "unbridled spirituality" is an appropriate way to think about biblical evangelism. We cannot witness to Jesus unless we know him and love him. We cannot tell others the story we do not really know for ourselves. We cannot speak of the transcendent meaning and purpose possible in a relationship with him unless we have experienced them ourselves. Unchurched people can spot the absence of genuineness at thirty paces. They know the difference between being handed a line and being given truthful testimony. The church that tries to witness without grounding its life in genuine spirituality cannot witness to the living waters of Jesus Christ. It can talk about the gospel, but it cannot witness to Jesus Christ.

If connectedness to Jesus is the foundation for intentional witnessing, the fruits of this experience are its motivation. Mainline churches that are spiritually alive cannot *not* witness. The passion to share the life they have in Jesus Christ cannot be hidden under a basket. In the experiential sense, this is a "realized eschatology" motivation for witnessing. When the church can say with the apostle Paul that we have been crucified with Christ, and it is no longer we who live, but Christ who lives in us (Galatians 2:20), then we have tasted the fruits of the reign of God. We do not have to wait for some future time. The time is now, and that is what makes us want to share this good news with others. We have life in Christ, and we want to tell our story in the hope of attracting someone else to want to have this life.

The urgency of this ministry grows from the conviction that the stakes are high. "Realized eschatology" is as much about life and death as "ultimate eschatology." Hell is not simply some distant place in a life beyond death. There is a here-and-now dimension to it that claims people's lives and robs them of meaning and purpose, hope and joy. These are not casual matters. They are matters of urgency. Churches that have experienced the power of life in Jesus Christ, the very life John's Gospel tells us we will find in him (20:31), will take evangelism seriously because they have a story to tell.

A study of the meaning of evangelism in the New Testament shows the biblical foundations for intentional witnessing. Michael Green notes three key words for evangelism: *euaggelizaesthai*—to tell; *kerussein*—to proclaim; and *marurein*—to bear witness.[2] Analysis of the words "telling" and "proclaiming" suggest they can be collapsed into the concept of "witnessing."[3] Several passages underscore the role of witnessing. In John's Gospel John the Baptist is described as a witness: "There was a man sent from God, whose name was John. He came as a witness to testify to the light, so that all might believe through him" (1:6–7). In making a defense of himself before the angry mob of Jews in Jerusalem, Paul tells his own story of becoming a Christian, recalling the fact that the Christian leader, Ananias, came to him and said, "The God of our ancestors has chosen you to know his will, to see the Righteous One and to hear his own voice; for you will be his witness to all the world of what you have seen and heard" (Acts 22:14–15).

During this same defense Paul says he spoke directly to Jesus and confessed that he had stood by and done nothing to help Stephen when he was being stoned to death, describing Stephen as a witness to Jesus (Acts 22:20). Luke tells us that after this defense, he appears before the Sanhedrin Council and angers them so much they have him thrown into prison, where Paul receives encouragement from Jesus himself, who tells him he must witness to the gospel in Rome: "That night the Lord stood near him and said, 'Keep up your courage! For just as you have testified for me in Jerusalem, so you must bear witness also in Rome'" (Acts 23:11). Further, Luke tells us Paul interprets his Damascus Road experience the same way to King Agrippa, telling the king that Jesus spoke to him directly and said, "I am Jesus whom you are persecuting. But get up and stand on your feet; for I have appeared to you for this purpose, to appoint you to serve and testify to the things in which you have seen me and to those in which I will appear to you" (Acts 26:15–16).

In John's Revelation a Christian martyr named Antipas is called a witness as the church at Pergamum is commended for its faithfulness: "You did not deny your faith in me even in the days of Antipas my witness, my faithful one, who was killed among you, where Satan lives" (2:13). So, too, is the church at Laodicea commended for being a faithful and true witness: "And to the angel of the church in Laodicea write: The words of the Amen, the faithful and true witness" (3:14).

A focus on the role of intentional witnessing is also found in the story in John's Gospel of Jesus' conversation with Nicodemus. Nicodemus tells Jesus he has come because he believes Jesus is "a teacher who has come from God; for no one can do these signs that you do apart from the presence of God" (John 3:2). Yet when Jesus begins to speak of such things as a new birth, of the work of the Holy Spirit in changing a person's life, turning it in another direction, Nicodemus protests that he doesn't understand. Jesus replies, "Very truly, I tell you, we speak of what we know and testify to what we have seen; yet you do not receive our testimony" (3:11). Jesus' words to Nicodemus offer an appropriate description of what happens in evangelism. We speak of what we know and testify to what we have seen. We tell what we believe about and what we experience in our personal and collective relationship with Jesus Christ. In this sense witness evangelism is incarnational. As Leander Keck has written, "The Flesh becomes word when we are grasped by the event of Jesus in such a way that we can bear witness to what we have seen in him, the historical Jesus."[4]

This is the meaning of the word "witness," one who has seen or heard something and can testify to it. Further, the Greek root of "witness" is *martus*, which means martyr, one who is willing to suffer death rather than renounce belief. The church's witness, therefore, is *to testify to the reality of its own growing conversion to Jesus Christ as Savior and Lord, risking everything in the process.* A witness does not bring another to believe her testimony, nor even to try to convince someone of the truth of her testimony. More than anything else, the reliability of the witness's character will be the deciding factor in whether her testimony is believed. Overt persuasion cannot convince someone a witness is telling the truth. The role of the witness is solely to tell the truth about what she has seen and heard. Whether or not the testimony is believed lies beyond her control.

Likewise, a church that preaches the gospel is one that tells the truth about its faith in and experience of the gospel. The quality of the church's character is the only thing it can do to make its testimony convincing. All the gimmicks and techniques of persuasion will not do it. The Spirit converts, but the Spirit needs testimony that is authenticated by the church's life and ministry.

Essentially, then, the ministry of intentional witnessing is a kind of teaching evangelism in which the church first of all embodies the ministry of Jesus. Effective teaching is not a process of persuading, but of telling and incarnating what is being taught. The church's character as a role model is a key factor in the ultimate effect "teaching" has. Most people remember teachers for who they were far more than for what they said. Their character often draws us to a subject as much as the subject itself.

For this reason evangelism as intentional witnessing can be likened to Ezekiel's call to prophesy to Israel. When the Spirit entered into Ezekiel and set him on his feet, positioning him to hear the call to prophesy, what he heard was this, "Whether they hear or refuse to hear (for they are a rebellious house), they shall know that there has been a prophet among them" (Ezekiel 2:5). The church makes a similar witness. Whether people hear or refuse to hear the witness, they will at least know that a witness has been among them. The result of the witness, its impact on others, is not the church's focus. That is in the hand of God. The church's role is testimonial.

When Jesus tells the disciples to go and baptize, he is telling the church to make an outward symbol of the Spirit's work. Paradoxically, baptism is itself the Spirit's work, deepening the experience of grace in both the new convert and the gathered community. In this sense baptism is a sacramental act of the church that both signals and confers the Spirit's work in the process of conversion. It is a commencement in the fullest sense of the beginning of a journey filled with joy and struggle.

This view of the ministry of evangelism is certainly not without precedent in the life of the church. A significant statement of intentional witnessing is the World Council of Churches document entitled *Mission and Evangelism—An Ecumenical Affirmation* approved by the WCC Central Committee in 1982. It is not practical to reprint the entire document here, so for our purposes I want to note several passages that underscore the church's evangelistic role as witness.

In the Preface, the statement declares:

> The Church is sent into the world to call people and nations to repentance, to announce forgiveness of sin and a new beginning in relations with God and neighbors through Jesus Christ. This evangelistic calling has a new urgency today.

> In a world where the number of people who have no opportunity to know the story of Jesus Christ is growing steadily, *how necessary it is to multiply the witnessing vocation of the church.*[5]

It goes on to speak of the essential task of sharing the good news of the reign of God; calling people to discipleship, service, and risk in a world where people are struggling for justice, freedom, and liberation; battling the modern-day demons of drugs and esoteric cults; and seeking to find meaning beyond the temporary security of their affluence.[6]

The Affirmation acknowledges that the starting point of the church's proclamation of good news is Jesus Christ, and him crucified. Thus, evangelism, it says, "calls people to look towards that Jesus and commit their lives to him, to enter into the kingdom whose king has come in the powerless child of Bethlehem, in the murdered one on the cross."[7]

In the section on ecumenical convictions the statement speaks to the issue of conversion:

> The proclamation of the gospel includes an invitation to recognize and accept in a personal decision the saving lordship of Christ. It is the announcement of a personal encounter, mediated by the Holy Spirit, with the living Christ, receiving his forgiveness, and making a personal acceptance of the call to discipleship and a life of service.[8]

The balancing of the role of the Holy Spirit with discipleship in the above quote witnesses to the need for grounding evangelism in faithfulness, something the Affirmation underscores earlier in declaring the need of the church to identify with all humanity in loving service and joyful proclamation:

> At the very heart of the church's vocation in the world is the proclamation of the kingdom of God inaugurated in Jesus the Lord, crucified and risen. Through its internal life of eucharistic worship, thanksgiving, intercessory prayer, through planning for mission and evangelism, through a daily lifestyle of solidarity with the poor, through advocacy even to confrontation with the powers that oppress human beings, the churches are trying to fulfill this evangelistic vocation.[9]

Evangelism and faithfulness are two sides of the same coin. Witnessing means identification with the poor and the confrontation of oppressive powers in all their forms, which is why in 1967 then-President Phillip Potter reminded the Central Committee meeting in Crete of the words of Dr. Visser't Hooft, who many years before had spoken prophetically when he said:

> The church which would call the world to order is suddenly called to order itself. The question it would throw into the world, "Do you know to whom you belong," comes back as an echo. The church discovers that it cannot truly evangelize, that its message is unconvincing unless it lets itself be transformed and renewed, unless it becomes what it believes it is.[10]

Because intentional witness evangelism balances mission and inward integrity, it is a ministry mainline churches can embrace for the sake of the world and for the sake of the church. It holds the power to bring about renewal in the church. This is because mainline churches need to see that their commitment to being faithful to the claims of the gospel is the key to their recovery of the ministry of evangelism, rooted in the desire to be "doers" of the Word, and not just hearers only (James 1:22). Granted, mainliners have been too guilty of compromising this commitment, but this does not change the fact that we have sought to be intentional in making membership integrity as important as membership growth. For this reason witness evangelism invites mainline churches to shed the doldrums we have wallowed in because of numerical decline and get on with being in the world as living reminders of Jesus Christ[11] in the confidence that being the biggest is not what the gospel is about. Being faithful is. As Lesslie Newbigin has put it:

> The real triumphs of the gospel have not been won when the church is strong in a worldly sense; they have been won when the church is faithful in the midst of weakness, contempt, and rejection. And I would simply add my own testimony, which could be illustrated by many examples, that it has been in

situations where faithfulness to the gospel placed the church in a position of total weakness and rejection that the advocate has himself risen up and, often through the words and deeds of very "insignificant" people, spoken the word that confronted and shamed the wisdom and power of the world.[12]

This is the foundation for evangelism. It is a ministry whose time has once again come because the church cannot be the church without intentionally witnessing to the truth that has transformed and is transforming its life. We have a story to tell, and we ought to learn how to tell it well, in preaching, teaching, identifying with the poor, and challenging the principalities and powers of the age. In the process the church certainly welcomes growth, even prays for it, but always as a by-product of conversion. The goal is membership only when it signals commitment to genuine discipleship.

NOTES

[1] Sally Morgenthaler, *Worship Evangelism* (Grand Rapids: Zondervan, 1995), p. 29.

[2] *Evangelism in the Early Church*, p. 49. (See note 30, ch. 2.)

[3] Ibid., p. 76. Green quotes in agreement the words of E. G. Selwyn: "I sometimes wonder whether the term 'kerygma' has not been worked too hard, and whether the word *marturia* and its cognates would not describe better the primitive and indispensable core of the Christian message." He then says, "Every initiative in evangelism recorded in Acts is the initiative of the Spirit of God" (p. 149). He further says that the early church "looked for a response" in the sense of asking people to decide for or against God (p. 151), but later in the book he explicitly says that this was not something quantifiable: "It is not possible to assess realistically the extent to which the evangelism of the early church was successful. For one thing, we have no means of comparing their 'successes' with their 'failures.' For another, God's assessment of success may differ greatly from our own, and as we have seen throughout this book, evangelism is supremely God's work…in which he enlists human cooperation" (p. 274).

[4] Leander E. Keck, "Evangelism in Theological Perspective," *Evangelism: Mandates For Action*, James T. Laney, ed. (New York: Hawthorn Books, Inc., 1975), p. 65.

[5] *Mission and Evangelism: An Ecumenical Affirmation: A Study Guide*, compiled by Jean Stromberg (Geneva: WCC, 1985), p. 1.

[6] Ibid.

[7] Ibid., p. 13.

[8] Ibid., p. 18. Later, it declares that "the call to conversion should begin with the repentance of those who do the calling, who issue the invitation" (p. 20), pointedly illustrated by the story of a young woman in Hong Kong who, despite her initial negative reaction to the Christians she first met, describes her experience by saying, "somehow I was gradually attracted by the life of the church" (p. 23). That is the method of witness evangelism: attraction.

[9] Ibid., p. 13.

[10] Quoted by John R. W. Stott, *Christian Mission in the Modern World* (Downers Grove: InterVarsity Press, 1975), p. 56.

[11] See Henri Nouwen, *The Living Reminder* (New York: Seabury, 1977).

[12] *The Open Secret*, p. 69. (See note 8, ch. 2.)

4

Becoming a Witness Evangelism Church

The last chapter called for mainline churches to reclaim the ministry of intentional witness evangelism. In one sense the call is misleading. It suggests evangelism is something we do, but that would be to misunderstand the basic nature of this ministry. Far from being something we do, evangelism is something we are. Unbridled spirituality is an action only because it is first a way of being. So to reclaim evangelism does not mean learning how to do it in a new way. It involves something far more radical than that. It means getting to the root of the problem that led us away from it in the first place. That problem is *spiritual stagnation*. This is the real enemy of evangelism. It is an enemy within, far more threatening than any danger from without. A contemporary word for spiritual stagnation is *ennui*, a kind of malaise, lethargy, that develops without much notice until it takes control. Ennui is a creeping disease, similar to the "frog in the kettle" effect. Drop a frog into boiling water and it will jump out. Let the heat slowly rise and the frog will stay in until it is boiled. That is how it is with ennui. It doesn't happen overnight. It comes on slowly, which is one reason why it is so dangerous. In the church ennui is spiritual stagnation.

In the New Testament it is described as a state of "lukewarmness." The church at Laodicea suffered from it: "And to the angel of the church in Laodicea write: The words of the Amen, the faithful and true witness, the origin of God's creation: 'I know your works; you are neither cold nor hot. I wish that you were either cold or hot. So, because you are lukewarm, and neither cold nor hot, I am about to spit you out of my mouth'" (Revelation 3:14–16). "Lukewarmness" is the biblical equivalent of ennui, or spiritual stagnation.

Though there are always exceptions, in general this is the state of mainline Protestantism. Though numerical decline is a concern, it is not what will determine the future of main-line churches. That remains in the hands of God, but in terms of the role we play in any future God grants, much will depend upon the state of our spiritual health. If mainline churches address this issue, witness evangelism will become a vital ministry once again. The reason is simple. The effectiveness of the witness of every church and every individual is always determined by their spiritual healthiness. Spiritually stagnated churches are ineffective witnesses to Jesus Christ because they stand empty-handed before people hungry for spiritual nurture. No one is attracted to a church that is spiritually sick. This is not to say that spiritually healthy churches always grow numerically. They may or may not. What matters is that they are spiritually healthy. Numerical growth is the work of the Holy Spirit. The point is not that growth is guaranteed if a church is spiritually healthy. Rather, it is that spiritually unhealthy churches cannot nurture current members or be an attracting witness to others. At best they struggle to hold on to the people they already have.

As obvious and widespread as spiritual stagnation is, it is not easy to admit that we suffer from it. We see it in other churches, but not in our own. We use euphemisms such as "being on a plateau" or "needing a shot in the arm." Seldom is spiritual stagnation actually named. The truth about ourselves we do not want to face is that we have become comfortable with "lukewarm" religion, not unlike the man sitting at the pool at Bethsaida for thirty-eight years whom Jesus asked if he really wanted to be healed (John 5:1–9). We say we want to have vital, alive congregations. We say we want to have growing churches. We say we want to be renewed. But do we, really? If so, why do we continue with business as usual?

There are signs of spiritual stagnation, subtle as they may be. The most common one is the "church work" mentality among mainliners. Lay ministry is defined almost exclusively as "church work," which means serving on a committee or a governing board, being elected to a church office, or being a member and/or officer in a church group of some kind, often out of a sense of duty or obligation. It is not uncommon to find laity serving on and even chairing committees or boards they do not want to be on. They serve because they think they should, and most clergy agree with them. The idea that they are ministers by virtue of their baptism is a concept they have never understood or taken seriously. They have little awareness of being engaged in the ministry of Jesus Christ. Ask people in First Church Anywhere if they consider themselves "called" into ministry, and almost without exception they will say "No." The concept of "call" they believe is important for their minister or priest is not something they associate with themselves. Their role is helping the minister do his or her ministry by serving a term in some position the church needs someone to fill. Many clergy are guilty of the same kind of truncated thinking about lay ministry. The best they do in equipping church members for ministry is to ask them to serve on a committee.

Another sign of spiritual stagnation is the fact that fun, food, and fellowship have become a steady diet in mainline churches. It is common for weekly schedules to revolve around spaghetti suppers, church bazaars, bake sales, rummage sales, and a host of other calendar stuffers that feed people on fun, food, and fellowship. My wife and I recently met several times with a group of young adults as an initial step in forming a group of their age to keep them connected to the church. In the second meeting we asked what they might want from the group, should it continue. The first response was, "I invited some of the other young adults in the church to this meeting, and I told them we weren't in to anything heavy, just fun, food, and fellowship." That is an exact quote. It is also what many churches try to provide because they are so spiritually stagnated they cannot give people anything else. Many ministers find it very difficult to schedule weekly Bible studies or other events directed at nurturing people spiritually. Matters are made worse by the fact that this emphasis on fun, food, and fellowship is often justified by the comment that people will not attend anything else, without any apparent awareness of what this says about the modern church.

It is no wonder that mainline churches are spiritually stagnated. When ministry is "church work," a matter of fulfilling a duty or obligation, and when churches offer little more than fun, food and fellowship, it is a clear sign that spiritual stagnation is winning the day. It is also an indication of the failure of mainliners to read the signs of the times. Whatever our view of the Promise Keepers movement,[1] when hundreds of thousands of men are willing to travel to Washington, D. C., to attend one of these events, as was the case recently, it is nothing short of a death wish for us to think that all people want from the church is fun, food, and fellowship, with a few programs thrown in. The time is ripe for the ministry of witness evangelism. From Promise Keepers to popular television programs about angels, the message is unmistakable. People are spiritually hungry.

Yet mainline churches remain tentative and slow in responding to the crisis. A man attending a workshop I was conducting at a mainline church came up afterward and asked, "When does a church member know when it is time to leave?" Unsure of what he was actually asking, I asked for clarification. He went on to explain that he was asking for help in knowing how to know when the time had come to give up on being spiritually fed in his church and simply go somewhere else. It was obvious leaving would be a painful decision for this man. Another man in the same workshop, much younger, asked why we didn't talk about spiritual issues very much in the church. Then he got very pointed and said that because I was a seminary teacher he wanted to ask me why ministers weren't preaching about spiritual things. When I asked what he meant by "spiritual things," he replied, "a personal relationship to Jesus, how to develop this relationship, and how to pray."

The concern these men were expressing points to the fact that mainline churches not only have lost members, but face the problem of many who still attend wanting help with their spiritual life but feeling that they are not getting it. We can dismiss their complaints as a sign of being unduly influenced by conservative theology, or we can hear them telling the truth about mainline church life—that we are bogged down in spiritual stagnation that hides itself in a flurry of activities and programs that spiritually is much ado about nothing.

I am willing to throw in my lot with the complainers. *I am convinced spiritual stagnation is why the ministry of evangelism has been neglected for so long.* Consciously or unconsciously we have known that we had little to share. It takes spiritual depth to make an authentic witness to discipleship that has the power to attract others to it. We know this is true when it comes to individuals. When Jean Vanier inaugurated the Harold M. Wit Lecture Series on Living a Spiritual Life in the Contemporary Age at Harvard University, he spoke to an overflow crowd.[2] Founder of L'Arche, Christian communities worldwide that provide a family-like environment where men and women with mental disabilities can gain a deeper sense of their own worth through loving relationships, Vanier is widely known as a man of spiritual depth and insight. This is the reason hundreds came to hear him speak. Not because of good publicity. Not because people wanted to learn how to start communities like L'Arche. They came because they knew they would be in the presence of a man of enormous spiritual power.

The same thing could be said of many others. During the tragedy of the Oklahoma City bombing in 1995, it was not surprising that evangelist Billy Graham was asked to speak to a grieving nation in the worship service held that weekend and broadcast nationwide. Words from someone widely considered to live close to God were needed. He was an obvious choice. I personally found his presence in that service amazingly calming to my own troubled spirit. More than his words, it was the spirit of the man himself that gave us comfort and strength. That is the way it is with people who live out of spiritual well-springs that run deep.

Churches are no different. When they live out of this kind of spiritual reservoir, they are empowered to make a winsome witness to others. This kind of passionate spirituality is possible for churches when they are what the apostle Paul described as the body of Christ: "Now you are the body of Christ and individually members of it" (1 Corinthians 12:27). These kinds of churches understand themselves as a living organism, not an organization, a community of faith to attend to, not a place to attend. They know their source of life is not themselves, but Jesus who is the head of the body, the One to whom they must remain connected, even as a branch is connected to a vine (John 15:1–5). Churches that live out of a passionate spirituality are by that very fact engaging in the ministry of witness evangelism. This is why, when we talk about this ministry, we are not talking about something churches do. We are talking about something they are. As the body of Christ, everything a church does in ministry witnesses to Jesus Christ. Thus, everything is evangelism. Reclaiming this ministry among mainline churches, therefore, means reclaiming the spiritual power to be the body of Christ in the world.

Steps to Becoming a Witness Evangelism Church

Below are steps that suggest a path mainline churches can follow that will lead to this end. I confess, however, that I say this with some anxiety. As a rule I find a "steps" approach to any problem personally a bit off-putting. One reason is the prescriptive tone it usually carries, which suggests that following certain steps will produce a predictable outcome. There is also the risk of churches deciding to follow these steps without really understanding all that is involved. Yet I have chosen to run the risk of these pitfalls in the hope of mapping out a strategy for mainline churches to reclaim evangelism and indirectly to address the serious problem of numerical decline. The steps are necessarily proactive, a way of trying to describe how to get from point A to point B. It is not so much the church's future that is on the line, but its soul. In an age of secularism, skepticism, and religious pluralism, mainline churches will continue to face a very uncertain future.[3] We cannot lose our heads in such a time as this, nor can we give up our integrity. The steps suggest a way to balance both.

Because my arena of ministry is the academy, it is also important to say that these are not steps that have never been tried, and certainly have not been tried and found wanting. In one form or another they have been culled from actual experience. In no instance of which I am aware have they ushered in a new era in a church's life, but they have made a difference. If they have in one church, they can in all churches.

STEP 1 ▬▬▬▬▬▬▬▬▬▬▬▬▬▬▬▬▬▬▬▬▬▬▬

Take a Year-long Congregational Sabbatical

Of Sabbath time Abraham Heschel writes:

> He [she] who wants to enter into the holiness of the day must first lay down the profanity of clattering commerce, of being yoked to toil. He [she] must go

away from the screech of dissonant days, from the nervousness and fury of acquisitiveness and the betrayal in embezzling his [her] own life. He [she] must say farewell to manual work and learn to understand that the world has already been created and will survive without the help of [humanity]. Six days a week we wrestle with the world, wringing profit from the earth; on the Sabbath we especially care for the seed of eternity planted in the soul. The world has our hands, but our soul belongs to Someone Else. Six days a week we seek to dominate the world; on the Seventh day we try to dominate the self.[4]

Sabbath rest is the stewardship of time. As Heschel points out, we live in and for the conquest of space, building, creating, toiling, all in an effort to subdue nature and garnish its yield for ourselves. Human beings are doers. We assess our worth by what we accomplish. The wrong in this is not our desire to produce, but our enslavement to it. In a culture of consumerism things now have dominion over us, whereas God intended it to be the other way around. We have forgotten that "it is not a thing that lends significance to a moment; it is the moment that lends significance to things."[5]

The Sabbath is helpful in understanding sabbatical time because Sabbath is the ritual of living into sacred activities as a way of learning to live life as a whole as sacred moments. It is, Dorothy Bass writes, "not just law and liturgy; it is also a shared way of life, a set of activities that becomes second nature...a piece of time that opens space for God."[6] Rooted in the tradition of Sabbath time, a congregational sabbatical invites mainline churches to reclaim their spiritual heritage of sacred time. It is a call to rest long enough to learn once again that life consists of much more than earning our way by the sweat of our brow. In the biblical story the holiness of time was established at the moment of creation: "And on the seventh day God finished the work that he had done, and he rested on the seventh day from all the work that he had done. So God blessed the seventh day and hallowed it, because on it God rested from all the work that he had done in creation" (Genesis 2:2–3). God fashioned Sabbath time as holy time in that we call to remembrance that we were born to delight in a creation that is good: "God saw everything that he had made, and indeed, it was very good" (Genesis 1:31).

The church is called to be a community of people who honor sacred time, who understand the importance of Sabbath rest, who know that life consists of more than the accumulation of things, more than the accomplishment of tasks, who know that spiritual strength is the strongest force in the world. But instead the church has become a reflection of the world. Uncomfortable with quiet, we grow anxious with waiting, and weary of praying. Our minds become restless, wondering, filled with things to do, places to go, people to see. We flit in and out of church meetings long enough to make our presence known. We serve only if things can get done, always assuming we know what those things are. We are quick to settle issues with a vote so we can move on to the next item on the agenda. In a church consumed by freneticism, like the world around us, Sabbath time is a call that strikes us as strange and impractical.

In a sermon in which Fred Craddock, one of the great preachers of today, addressed the issue of ennui or spiritual stagnation among ministers, he suggested that before they throw in the towel and go running off to a career counselor, they go to bed.[7] Excellent advice, I would say. Rest has a way of clearing the mind and restoring the soul—"he leads me beside still waters, he restores my soul" (Psalm 23:2b–3a). That is the purpose of a sabbatical leave. It is not a vacation. It is rest, a withdrawal from routine for the sake of inward nourishment. I am writing these words during such a sabbatical from my teaching responsibilities. The most accurate summary of what it has meant to have this time are the words, "Don't just do something, stand there." That is what a sabbatical is. It is consciously disengaging from all the stuff one is doing and simply standing there, being there. Sabbatical symbolizes the human need for spiritual replenishment, for renewal and rest from normal activities. It is a more extended version of a Sabbath day.

Churches need sabbaticals as much as individuals. Spiritual stagnation deepens in the soil of freneticism. A congregational sabbatical can be a time for nurturing spiritual roots, a time for slowing down and taking the time to listen, to pray, and to learn. But it means just what it says—taking a sabbatical from the routine and schedules that define a church's life. The usual work of committees and departments is suspended, especially the development of programs. Only the bare essentials to keep the machinery going are maintained during sabbatical time. The governing body can attend to necessary business, but this, too, needs to be kept at a minimum. Established groups, such as church school classes, women's and men's groups should also be involved in sabbatical time, either by choosing not to meet or focusing their time on prayer and study. The point is to step away from customary activity. Renewal will not occur if the old routine is maintained. It would be like a teacher taking a sabbatical but continuing to teach. It is the break from routine that helps to create the space for something new to emerge.

During the congregational sabbatical, the formation of what I call Spiritual Life Groups (SLGs) can be a helpful way to nurture personal and collective spirituality. These are small groups of eight to ten people that focus on (1) prayer, (2) study, (3) community building, and (4) dreaming great dreams for the congregation. The ministers and a small group of lay leaders meet to organize the makeup of the groups. Geographical location is one of the easiest ways by which to divide membership. People should be given the opportunity to attend a different group if attending the one to which they have been assigned proves to be a problem.

The SLG meetings need to be weekly and structured in the following way: A significant portion of each meeting should be spent in prayer and worship. This time can be led by a different person each meeting, or only those who are willing to volunteer to do it. Silence should be observed in every meeting. I recommend, in fact, that every meeting begin with five or ten minutes of silence before anything is said. Members should know that at the appointed hour to begin the group enters into silence. It is broken by the person who is leading worship. Each meeting should also end with a time of intercessory prayer.

In between the times of prayer and worship members share their spiritual autobiography. Most churches have been too busy to take the time to ask people to tell them the story of the spiritual influences and experiences that have brought them to where they are. Having done this for twenty years, I can assure any church that there is a treasury of inspiration waiting to be released through these stories. The storyteller shares uninterrupted. No questions are asked, no comments made. This is a chance to hear how God has worked in the lives of people we don't know and people we think we know very well. It is an experience that will enrich the faith of every participant.

Once all the members have shared their spiritual autobiographies, the group begins a study of a book previously selected by the minister and lay leaders group.[8] The important thing is not to make this a purely intellectual exercise. Understanding is important, but the need is to hear the word of the Lord in the study. For this reason two questions should guide the discussion: "What helps me personally in this chapter?" "How does this chapter speak to our church?" What needs to be avoided is a debate about the merits of the ideas in the book. The two questions will get at this concern while keeping the focus of the group's time on spiritual growth and nurture. These questions help the group focus on personal and collective spiritual needs.

It is, of course, essential during this sabbatical time that all members commit themselves to daily disciplined spiritual nurture. One of the realities that has to be faced is that the church alone cannot meet people's spiritual needs. Members must take responsibility for their own spiritual health. They cannot expect SLGs to do what they have to do for themselves. It is the combination of personal and collective spiritual nurture that builds a strong witnessing community.

At the end of three months I recommend that the membership in the SLGs change. The last meeting of all the groups is centered on celebrating the gift of time together. The group ends its life when the last meeting concludes. Two weeks later new groups are formed in the same way as before, and a new book is selected for study. This is repeated again after six months. Then at the end of nine months new groups are formed, but with a different agenda. Whereas the discussion in the groups during the first nine months will obviously overflow into various subjects related to spirituality, church life, and other concerns, during this last quarter the concepts described in the remainder of the steps below become the focus, as well as the proposal for restructuring congregational life presented in Chapter 6. The goal is not adoption of the concepts, but an open and honest examination of them. This quarter would conclude with a worship service in which members would sign the TEAM Covenant to be explained in Step 2.

Sabbatical time is a practical way to step back and live deeper into the Spirit in the trust that new life will emerge. It brings intentionality to spiritual growth. At a time when mainline churches have either grown complacent about evangelism or have gone running after the latest program that promises numerical growth, sabbatical time calls them back to basics, that which informs and forms their life together in Jesus Christ. Churches willing to slow down and spend time in prayer and study will see a significant strengthening of their spiritual life. They will learn the meaning of the words, "...but those who wait for the LORD shall renew their strength, they shall mount up with wings like eagles, they shall run and not be weary, they shall walk and not faint" (Isaiah 40:31).

STEP 2

Identify the Congregation's Core Beliefs and Values

In recent years denominations have encouraged churches to write a mission statement as a means of clarifying what they should be doing, to bring some focus to their ministry as they do some long-range planning for the future. Without intending to do so, this puts the cart before the horse. Before a congregation determines its mission, it needs to clarify its identity. The church has a distinctive identity as a called community. As members we are not free to do whatever we want to do. We are free to do what we discern Jesus calling us to do in the particular social/cultural/economic/political context in which we find ourselves. Every congregation needs to be as specific as it can be in understanding its identity. What it does should issue from who it is.

One of the weaknesses of mainline churches is losing focus on what makes them who they are. This happens in part because of *enculturation*, which is the inordinate influence of cultural values on the church.[9] To a degree greater than we want to admit, money, power, and prestige that define success in America also define it in the church. Despite our claims that fundamentalists blur the distinctions between Christianity and Americanism, mainliners are in bondage to the dominant culture as much as anyone. Moreover, it is a bondage of consent. It is this state of enculturation that in large measure accounts for why mainliners talk about spiritual stagnation, but do little about it.

None of us in the church, of course, escape the influence of the dominant culture. But a lack of awareness of its negative influences is the real danger. It is not only the presence of enculturation in the church that does the damage. It is the fact that its influence goes unnoticed. Many churches make decisions out of an encultured value system without realizing what they are doing. Thirteen-million-dollar complexes are built to the glory of God in a world where three-fifths of the population live in poverty. Ministers seek positions that pay high salaries, yet bemoan the materialism that is corrupting the morals and ethics of the young. Search committees and bishops look for ministers who have an ability to manage before they examine the candidate's capacity to care for others. Economic, social, political, racial, gender, and sexual barriers that determine who is in and who is out in the larger society play a major role in the attitudes and actions found in many churches.

Willimon and Hauerwas tell a story about a young pastor who was an advocate for a day-care center in the church he served at a meeting of the Christian education committee. He listed several reasons why this was a good proposal: The church had the facilities; it would be an example of good stewardship of the building for it to be used this way; it might serve to bring new members in; it was a way to engage in social mission in the community. Despite the strength of the pastor's argument, one of the committee members, a woman named Gladys, questioned the wisdom of the center. When another committee member tried to make the case for the day-care center serving the needs of families who were financially strapped, Gladys spoke even more passionately against it. She said there certainly were people in their city who had real financial need, and she would be willing to do something to help them. But she contended they would not be the ones to use the proposed day-care center. They wouldn't even have a way to get their children to the church. Gladys was convinced the day-care center would serve people for whom she believed it was becoming financially harder every day to have two cars, a VCR, a place at the lake, or a motor home. "That's why we're all working hard and leaving our children," she said. "I just hate to see the church buy into and encourage that value system.…This day-care center will encourage some of the worst aspects of our already warped values."

The pastor could have been upset with Gladys. Instead,

however, he responded with wisdom beyond his years when he said, "Gladys, with questions like the ones you are raising, we just might become church after all."[10]

Clarifying our peculiar identity as the body of Christ can help unmask the effects of enculturation and also provide a buffer to its influence. The place to begin is to name our core beliefs and values. The book *Built to Last*, by James Collins and Jerry Porras, documents how essential preserving core beliefs and values is to the mission of a group. They compare eighteen of the top American corporations that are what they call "visionary companies," those that set the standard for all the rest, with eighteen good companies, but not leaders in their field. The average age of these corporations was one hundred years. They discovered that one of the central factors in the durability of the visionary companies was their ability to maintain their "core ideology." This consisted of two things: (1) a "core philosophy"; and (2) core values. The eighteen visionary companies had learned how, in the words of the authors, to "preserve the core." They held firm to their core philosophy, ideals, beliefs, and values.[11]

Many churches do not know what their core beliefs and values are, and, thus, they confuse what is essential to maintain and what is not, as well as being more vulnerable to beliefs and values of the dominant culture. Mission statements have only exacerbated this problem by naming what a church does before identifying the basic beliefs and values that make a church what it is. Means have now become ends. We make how we do something more important than why we're doing it. An identity statement is a tangible way to refocus on what it truly means to be the church. The standard for how we do anything should be the degree of its effectiveness in expressing the core values that guide and shape the group's life. Let me draw upon the place where I serve to illustrate this principle.

At our seminary we say that one of our core values is collegiality. One of the ways this gets expressed is through the process we follow in calling new faculty members. A committee of the faculty screens names, and brings the three top candidates to campus for interviews with the entire faculty and representatives from the student body. The students give feedback to the faculty regarding their impressions of all three. Finally the faculty votes to recommend one person to the president, who then recommends that person to the trustees. This is a shared governance approach, yet the school's founding charter gives sole power to the president, upon trustee approval, to appoint new faculty. But to function that way would violate one of the core values that has sustained the seminary for many years.

That is how values influence the way a group gets things done. Identity determines process. Mission statements, on the other hand, do not raise this kind of issue. Sabbatical time is a marvelous opportunity for churches to identify their core values and beliefs, and then ask if the current structure really embodies them. If, for example, a church believes in justice seeking as a primary mark of its identity, then a social action committee may be an inadequate way to make this kind of witness. If a church is predominately white but believes racial diversity is a gift from God, then the process in the by-laws for filling leadership positions may not serve this purpose and could, in fact, thwart it. Without this kind of work on identifying core beliefs and values, churches will continue to let how they do things unduly influence what they do. In other words, they will continue to let the tail wag the dog. Reestablishing our identity can be a helpful step toward turning this around.

A simple exercise to do this is for members of Spiritual Life Groups to identify by means of consensus what they believe are the congregation's five core beliefs and five core values. The ministerial staff and lay leaders might identify several in advance (25–30) from which each group may choose or come up with others. Then all the groups gather to hear a report from each group. The top ten beliefs and values are written down, and an attempt to reach a final agreement on the top five is made through the same process. My wife and I have used this exercise with churches, and the results have been quite revealing and helpful.

Once the core beliefs and values of the congregation are identified, a TEAM Covenant can be developed. This is a simple statement that describes the need for every member making a commitment of Time, Energy, Attention, and Money as expressions of their devotion to Jesus Christ and the church that bears his name and lives by his power. The Covenant is then signed and taken home as a reminder of the commitment to discipleship each member has made.

STEP 3

Start Changing What Is Non-core

The authors of *Built to Last* also noted that visionary companies not only learned how to "preserve the core," but how to balance that by "stimulating progress." This meant that everything beyond core ideology was subject to change. They quote Sam Walton, the founder of Wal-Mart, who said, "You can't just keep doing what works one time, because everything around you is always changing. To succeed, you have to stay out in front of that change."[12] Businesses, of course, have no choice but to change. Their survival depends on it.

The church is not a business, of course, and never should be, but the irony is that many businesses know more about what is core and what is non-core than a lot of churches. This accounts for one of the reasons churches resist necessary changes. They cling to what is non-core and in the process lose what is. What becomes sacred is how things are done, rather than what is being done. In my own tradition, for example, sharing the Lord's supper weekly is a core belief that reflects the core value we have of the community being formed around the table. How it is done or when it occurs in the worship service is not core. Yet both "how" and "where" have been points of tension and division in many of our churches. We have not learned what is core and what is not. Thus we fear that in changing our ways of doing things we will lose our identity.

What mainline churches fail to see is that there is a direct correlation between resisting changing and spiritual stagnation. A church that spiritually nurtures its members is a church that is not afraid to change. The need is not for churches to face the reality of a changing world. The need is for them to change. Facing change suggests coping with that which comes from the outside. Changing, on the other hand, has to do with what is happening on the inside. Here we see the relationship between change and sabbatical time. It takes spiritual maturity to change. Fear and unreasoned resistance to change are signs of spiritual immaturity. They reveal a basic insecurity precisely because churches have sought security in what is not core rather than what is.

Consequently, they lack the spiritual maturity to engage in a ministry of witness evangelism. The issue is not what to change. That depends on many variables. The issue is our attitude toward changing. The courage to change is a sign of spiritual power, and that in itself is a winsome witness to the gospel. Mainliners must face the truth about themselves. This is why Sabbath time can help churches make changes. It renews their spirit and, thus, their courage. We cannot keep saying we want renewal and then refuse to change anything that might stand in the way of reaching that goal. Our spiritual well-being is at stake.

STEP 4

Confront the Tyranny of the Minority

This step has to be paired with the preceding one. While the majority in any church needs to be sensitive to the concerns of the minority, one of the primary reasons mainline churches don't change is the opposite problem—the tyranny of the minority. It only takes a few people to resist change for a church to remain spiritually stagnant. Clarification of core beliefs and values will help overcome this resistance, but there will always be those people who would rather see their church die than change. Though their numbers are usually not large, they can exercise tyrannical power through intimidation, unsubstantiated claims of large numbers of people being upset, and grapevine gossip. Add the conspiracy of silence among the majority that is so common in churches, and the tyranny of the minority exists without challenge. For years I have witnessed this tyranny in small churches served by students. It does not matter how qualified a woman or minority candidate might be, if a few resist them because of gender or race, though they know it is wrong, the majority will acquiesce.

This is a serious problem. The empirical evidence is rather overwhelming in its conclusions. Those churches that resist change die. It's the dinosaur effect. That which does not adapt dies. The deteriorating church buildings lining the streets of urban centers are a testimony to this reality. Change alone would not have saved them, but resistance to change took away any chance for renewal they had. This problem is exacerbated by the lack of courage among ministers to confront the issue. Worried about being terminated, and having to deal with antagonistic people, they abandon leadership responsibilities, hang on as long as they can, and then retire or move to another place of ministry.

Sabbatical time can help churches confront this tyranny because it is a chance to ground themselves in a biblical understanding of church and ministry, to pray without ceasing to the point where they experience the infusion of the power of the Holy Spirit, thereby learning to put their trust in God alone. When this happens, those who resist change at all costs will be exposed for what they are doing. Change for the sake of change offers nothing to churches, but neither does resistance for the sake of resistance. The issue is whether or not a church wants to witness to the gospel, which is timeless, in ways that are always changing.

STEP 5

Build a Bridge Between Church Membership and Discipleship

When the church gained legitimacy in the empire early in the fourth century, its relationship to the larger culture underwent radical transformation. When being a Christian became a necessity for survival in the empire by the end of that century, discipleship and church membership became bifurcated. The church has struggled since that time to unite the two. There are ways congregations can do it, but that it must be done is no longer an option for churches desirous of spiritual renewal.

There are two ways churches can enhance the possibility that membership truly will be discipleship. The first is a series of required courses that are prerequisites for membership, which explain what membership really means. Churches that allow people to join without consultation with the ministerial staff should make continuation of membership conditional upon completion of this study. A suggested curriculum might include the following classes: (1) an introduction to the Bible; (2) an introduction to the nature of the church and its ministry, including the meaning of baptism as "ordination" to the priesthood of all believers; (3) an introduction to classical spiritual disciplines; (4) an overview of church history, including a review of the congregation's own history and denominational identity; (5) a class explaining the church's TEAM Covenant (Time, Energy, Attention, Money) as described in Step 2, concluding with the signing of this covenant in the context of worship. A minimum of six hours should be devoted to the first three classes, three to the fourth one, and one to the fifth—a total of twenty-two hours of study.

The second step would be to make a year's membership in a Spiritual Life Group, explained in Step 1, a requirement. This would provide help to new members in areas such as practicing spiritual disciplines, discovering spiritual gifts, and discerning the ministry group they would join upon leaving the SLG (see Chapter 6). The permanent establishment of an SLG ministry will require the minister to take responsibility for leading the group until it becomes a ministry for which a group of laity is willing to take responsibility. At that point the members of the ministry group would lead SLGs for new members.

This two-step process for church membership offers a tangible way to unite membership and discipleship. The first objection to it, of course, will be that churches will lose potential members. The irony is that the opposite turns out to be the case. That is, the greater the standard, the higher people will reach. Churches that have risked asking for greater commitment have discovered that they usually get it.[13] Mainline churches have tended to ask too little from people rather than too much. Church membership that counts for little or has no accountability attracts few and holds on to even fewer. Requiring people to understand what they are getting into is not a deterrent. It says you know what you're doing and you want them to know. People who don't want to take the time to learn about a church and don't want to have any expectations of them if they join are not serious about Christian discipleship. Why lower membership standards to make it easier for this kind of person to fall over the threshold? High standards often meet with a high response. People respect quality. Mainline churches that want to be effective witnesses to the gospel will have to take the difficult step of reestablishing the integrity of church membership.

Scripture makes it very clear that the bifurcation of membership and discipleship is unacceptable in the body of Christ. Need we be reminded of the words of the letter of James to be doers of the word and not hearers only (James 1:22)? Jesus obviously expected the same thing from us. Why else would he have said that not everyone who calls him Lord will enter the reign of God, but only those who follow the will of God

(Matthew 7:21)? The NIV translation of James 1:22 is as pointed as these words of Jesus: "Do not merely listen to the word, and so deceive yourselves. Do what it says." But Jesus adds an important element to living the word we say we believe in. He promises that those who do will discover that their lives are built on a solid foundation (Matthew 7:24–27). In other words, they will learn that their true security is in their relationship to him. Here is the motivation for taking the relationship between belief and action seriously. It is how we experience what it means to live in the world but not be of it. Spiritual stagnation is born of the church's failure to live this way. Being a member of the church does not nurture spiritual growth. Belonging to Jesus Christ does. Membership can symbolize this, but it cannot be a substitute for it.

STEP 6

Make Decisions by Consensus

The Quaker process of decision making by consensus seems impractical to many mainliners, but I suggest that implementing it is one of the primary changes needed in mainline church life. Majority decision making by vote is an extremely negative influence on the spiritual life of any congregation. When the church votes, nobody wins; everyone loses. A voting church is like a person whose body parts vote to work or not work. Majority rule is a shortcut way to make decisions that relieve mainline churches of the responsibility to seek the Spirit guidance by waiting. Voting is a sign of impatience. Too many mainline ministers and church members would rather "call for the question" than to pray and wait. Thus majority rule both symbolizes and perpetuates mainline spiritual stagnation.

Consensus building, on the other hand, offers churches a practical way to grow in the Spirit. The process works precisely in the way the name implies. When the body has to make a decision, it seeks to gain a consensus for that decision.

The process begins with prayer. Only then are views shared. The point is that time is taken for the group to sense where the Spirit is leading it. Only when consensus is reached is the decision implemented. Reaching consensus may involve the practice of "stepping aside." This means if the will of the group is clearly discernible, the few who do not agree accept the group's will and agree to step aside to make consensus possible. This is more than simply "getting out of the way." Because their views have been heard, the process has been deliberate and fair, and the group has sought the leading of the Spirit in its decision, those who disagree are expected to support the decision. They do not work in opposition, nor do they secretly hope for the group to fail. They work for the common good, in spite of their failure to agree with the decision. In the context of consensus building, the group has no choice but to be open to the leading of the Spirit. In this way the process itself strengthens the spiritual life of a church. In addition, votes may be taken at a certain point in a discussion, but only as a way to determine if consensus has been reached.

Clearly consensus building requires a high level of spiritual maturity, yet it also contributes to this maturity. It does not allow churches to take the quick and easy, albeit destructive, way out. Moreover, consensus building connects issues of governance to the life of the Spirit. In a time when voting has become more and more divisive among mainline churches, consensus building offers a fresh approach to decision making that does not avoid confronting issues. It simply slows down the process. It may require more time than following Robert's Rules of Order, but it is much more consistent with being the body of Christ. I speak from experience when I say that consensus building can work. The Quakers, of course, have a long tradition of making decisions this way. So the issue is not whether consensus building will work. It is a matter of whether or not we are willing to trust the Spirit to lead us.

STEP 7

Make Worship a Spiritually Nurturing Experience

Worship is the center of any congregation's life. It is the most important moment a church experiences weekly because it is that time when the community gathers to praise God collectively, to hear the Word proclaimed collectively, and to break bread, to witness baptisms, to celebrate ministries, all done in community. Worship is so important because it is the most important thing a church does as a community to build itself spiritually. That is what worship must do—spiritually build the church. The only worship that is worthy of God is that which strengthens people's connectedness to Jesus. Let me be clear about what is not being said here. Spiritually strengthening worship does not mean an order or lack thereof that people like. It does not mean a good or not so good choir. It does not mean singing familiar hymns or new praise songs. It does not mean following or not following a particular tradition or participating in particular sacramental acts and rituals. It does not mean liking or not liking the preacher's sermons. It does not mean always leaving with a good feeling. What it does mean is that God is praised, the presence of Jesus is celebrated, and the Word that comforts and afflicts is proclaimed. All the other things mentioned have a place, but they are always and only the means to an end.

When the focus of worship is God, and the name of Jesus who reveals God is praised, then, as Sally Morgenthaler argues, by its very nature worship becomes evangelism. She makes a compelling case that worship is the key to every church's life, mainline and non-mainline alike: "Worship, both personal and corporate, feeds and sustains the body of Christ in a way nothing else can do."[14]

Most mainliners would agree. The real debate swirls around the kind of worship to have. Traditionalists and innovators find themselves locked in uncompromising positions on this issue. While my personal experience convinces me that spiritually nurturing worship wears more than one stripe, the basic problem in this debate is the "either-or" attitude of both sides. They have concluded that worship has to be one way or the other, traditional or contemporary, hymns or praise songs, innovative or prayer book. What they fail to understand is that sustained vitality in any group is possible only when "either-or" thinking is replaced with a "both-and" attitude.[15] To argue that only one form of worship can be spiritually nurturing, besides being embarrassingly arrogant, limits the ways in which the Holy Spirit can work among us. The key to any worship experience is that God is worshiped, and that lives are genuinely changed, that transformation happens, not because of tradition or gimmicks, but because the Spirit is present.[16]

"Either-or" thinking thrives in congregations that forget a simple theological principle. We praise God because God is the One we are seeking to please. Many mainline churches are bogged down in "either-or" debates about worship because of the mistaken notion that its sole focus is to please the congregation. Too often what is acceptable and unacceptable in worship is determined by people's likes and dislikes. One would hope that worship would be pleasing to worshipers, but when that is the main criterion, it degenerates into self-indulgence by the majority. The hope for mainliners thinking about forms of worship with a "both-and" attitude lies in the recognition that what we are about is pleasing God, not ourselves. Many Roman Catholic parishes are demonstrating the fruits of this kind of attitude. Their services blend traditional and contemporary music, ritual with innovation, even as they have shown with the success of the Saturday evening Mass that the Sunday morning worship hour is not sacrosanct. The fact that mainliners continue to be embroiled in controversy over these same matters suggests we have a long way to go in understanding what is core and what is not in the life of our churches.

More than anything else, regardless of the form of worship, the experience has to be rooted in genuine faith.

Worship does not give us faith. It expresses it. Worship is one of the fundamental ways a congregation witnesses. That is why worship is evangelism. Says Morgenthaler, "our failure to impact contemporary culture is not because we have not been relevant enough, but because we have not been real enough. Real faith witnesses."[17] I believe this is the key to the power of the worship experience among African-American churches. The Spirit-led singing and preaching so evident are rooted in real faith. The people are not maintaining tradition at all costs, nor are they employing gimmicks to create an effect. African-American worship expresses the real faith of the people. That is the source of their vitality.

This need for worship to be rooted in real faith has a direct bearing on the issue of forms of worship among mainliners. Diversity of forms does not mean we can be something we are not. It is a painful experience when we try to be. Recently a gathering of mainline churches included a group from a non-mainline church that had been invited to lead a workshop on new worship forms. The "worship team" from this church came fully equipped with instruments, songs, and their particular ethos as a faith community. What they demonstrated was what they experienced as meaningful worship. It fit who they were as the body of Christ in their community. But it was obvious that their music and accompanying theology did not "fit" those gathered. It was like apples and oranges trying to be the same fruit. While new forms of worship are appealing to a broad spectrum of Christian communities, churches must be careful to assure that what they are doing matches who they are. That is the only way worship can nurture people's spiritual needs and strengthen the ministry of witness evangelism.

What every mainline church must face if it desires to witness, or even to have any life about it at all, is that vital worship life is the lifeblood of its corporate life. Those who say dead worship simply reflects an already dead church may be correct, but I am convinced that many mainline congregations are staying alive *in spite of* their corporate worship life. But in the long run it is a losing battle. That one survey after another tells us the majority of the people who attend mainline churches find worship boring should concern us. One survey reported that baby boomers list boring worship as the number two reason they do not attend church.[18] Perhaps the attitude reflected in these surveys is simply consumeristic and, thus, not worth worrying about? But I think that is to take the easy way out. My personal experience is that worship often is boring because it offers no substantive food for mind or heart. No mainline church that wants to witness can be complacent about worship. The issue is not whether it effectively attracts new people, but whether or not it feeds those who already attend. This is why declining worship attendance is sufficient cause for examining what we are doing. It does little good in the long run to try to appeal to people not attending while those who do leave hungry every week. To think the problem always lies with the individual who is critical of mainline worship or who simply drops out is to bury our heads in the sand. Worse, it is a form of selfishness. Worship is not simply for the majority. It is for the community called the body of Christ.

Amid all the things that mainline churches must confront about their worship life, I am convinced the one factor that stands out from all the rest is spectatorship. Nurturing worship is participatory. A congregation of spectators who watch what is being done will never have the kind of worship that spiritually builds the church. This is why the so-called "contemporary" worship services mainliners are trying today will not in themselves solve the problem.[19] They, too, encourage spectator worship, adding to an already performance-focused experience. It is not simply the kind of music sung, for example, but who does the singing. Congregational participation is a critical factor in the kind of worship churches need today. Spectator worship discourages church members from thinking about their own ministry, or about the fruit and gifts of the Spirit they embody. Spiritually nurturing worship invites people to participate in celebration of the ways they and their church witness to Jesus Christ. Nothing can substitute for worship that builds up the church.

STEP 8

Value the Stewardship of Preaching

This step seems to be primarily for ministers, but laity also need to listen to the conversation. They play more of a role in good preaching than many of them realize. In recent years the pulpit has begun to make a comeback from the dark days of the late sixties and early seventies when preaching was considered dead. But there is still a lot of dead preaching around that is killing the church. Preaching is not everything, but it is a lot more than many mainline ministers are giving to it and through it. Preaching is that moment when a minister has the responsibility to speak words the Holy Spirit might use to become the word of life to someone listening. The pulpit is that marvelous opportunity to teach people what the gospel means for their daily lives. Here the fruit and the gifts of the Spirit can be explained, calls to discipleship and ministry nourished and strengthened, and the prophetic critic that exposes idolatry in the church and in the world can be offered. Preaching is a chance to make the Bible come alive for the laity as they are drawn into its stories and begin to see how their lives and the living word intersect.

A church that has weak preaching will almost always be a church in which spiritual stagnation weakens its ability to witness through its life and ministries. While the sixteenth-century Reformation leader Martin Luther didn't address the problem of "poor" preaching, he did speak to the indispensability of it in worship when he said: "Know first of all that a Christian congregation should never gather together without the preaching of God's word....When God's Word is not preached, one had better neither sing nor read, or even come together."[20]

In general laity are generous in their tolerance of poor preaching. This is not helpful. While it may be true that not every minister has the spiritual gift for preaching, every minister can be a good steward of this responsibility, and congregations must play a role in holding them accountable for doing so. When it is obvious the stewardship is being neglected, and it will be obvious, lay leadership must address the issue with the minister. At the same time, church members need to realize that they cannot expect to have good preaching when they are not willing to honor the time it takes for preparation. Being a good pastor is important, but not at the expense of sermon preparation. Congregations must face up to the fact that they cannot expect good preaching unless they are willing to affirm the need for the prayer and study that make it possible.

Good preaching only underscores the importance of worship in the life of a church. Somewhere along the way many mainline ministers became convinced that preaching gets in the way of "real" worship. Nothing could be further from the truth. People appreciate every other part of worship even more when they hear sermons that have depth of content and spirit and are delivered with sufficient passion that demonstrates the preacher actually believes what is being said. There is no tension between worship and preaching except in the mind of the preacher who is a poor steward of it. Preaching is a holy moment in the life of a church. Every minister and every congregation ought to be good stewards of it.

STEP 9

Reestablish the Church's Teaching Ministry

The rise of spiritual stagnation in mainline churches has been commensurate with the decline in their ministry of Christian education. I believe there is reason to think a causal relationship exists between the two. At the very least it can be said with confidence that education offers a rich opportunity for Christians to be nurtured spiritually. Moreover, an effective educational ministry has a direct bearing on the effectiveness of a ministry of witness evangelism. Here, again, ministers have a key role to play. They are called to equip the laity for ministry. Some mainline ministers are taking this responsibility seriously. Recently I received a newsletter from a church publicizing a spiritual formation study the associate pastor was planning to begin and a study of spiritual gifts the pastor had already begun. This is the kind of leadership mainline congregations need if they are to do effective ministry that forms the core of witness evangelism. In too many instances the teaching ministry of mainline clergy has been sacrificed in the name of administrative and pastoral care/counseling responsibilities. Heeding Westerhoff's call for "evangelization" and "catechesis"[21] rest primarily on the shoulders of mainline clergy.

So important is education in overcoming spiritual stagnation that I believe every mainline church needs to become a mini-seminary. In some instances several churches may join efforts in this regard. Seminary education today is much more than the acquisition of skills, as important as these are. It involves information and formation. Students are in the same process as everyone else. They are moving from becoming Christians to becoming Christian. While it is a lifelong process, a certain level of maturity must be achieved at the end of their study if they are to be ready to help others grow. We say to our students that seminary education involves learning how to do some things in ministry (skills), learning how to think theologically about those things (information), and learning how to become a minister (formation).

These three dimensions of education must also be attended to in congregations that want to nurture their members spiritually. The quality of the witness of any church will be determined by the degree to which this kind of education is taking place. It is for this reason that the decline of adult education among mainline churches today is to be viewed with alarm. Sunday "church school" is nearly dead in most mainline churches, without any sustainable educational structure to take its place. It is not uncommon for attendance at Sunday and/or weekday church school to be a third or less than worship. This means the majority of worshipers on a given Sunday in most mainline churches are receiving no formal educational instruction or formation. It is no wonder that people come to worship only if they "enjoy" it. Bereft of any theological understanding of the meaning of worship or its constitutive parts, they are left with no other basis upon which to make a decision. The same thing can be said about decision making. Church members vote things up or down according to their personal opinion without any substantive knowledge of what scripture or their church tradition might say about the issue.

This kind of thing has to be stopped. The ability and credibility of the witness of mainline congregations is at stake. A few mainline churches have developed effective weekday curricula approaches to education for their members, extensive formation classes for new converts and prospective members, and workshop and retreat experiences that draw upon outside resources. These are more the exception than the rule, however, and even in these churches in-depth study of scripture plays a small role. This is disturbing. Knowledge and understanding of the Bible is the most important educational task a church has. Today it is the area of study suffering the most. Adult classes organized around a book or topical discussion bristle or shrug at the suggestion that they study the Bible.

If adult education is essential for adequate spiritual nurture in many mainline churches, educating our children in the faith is an even greater need. Studies have clearly established the fact that passing the tradition on to our children is indispensable for the health and well-being of any church, not to speak of its numerical growth or decline.[22] While children's education is the last vestige of Sunday morning education in most mainline churches, the quality of this ministry remains a challenge. Children are often taught by teachers who themselves feel inadequately prepared and even caught by circumstances that force them to continue teaching when they want and need relief. Attendance is sometimes sporadic because of the failure of parents to be sufficiently interested in bringing their children on a regular basis. And then there is the problem of curriculum that challenges the best teacher to adapt it to fit the needs of the children and the abilities of the teacher. The real question, however, is "How do mainliners teach children faith in the context of extreme relativism that has undermined any basis for authority?"

The task of educating our children is a daunting one, but it is also an essential one for the spiritual health of mainline churches. Further, it is a responsibility any church can fulfill, if it has sufficient commitment to it. Such a church knows that children are life-giving to a community of faith. They bring spontaneity, innocence, and inquisitiveness, all of which create an environment that nurtures everyone's spirit. It is no wonder that Jesus invited children to be with him and warned us not to neglect them or lead them astray (Matthew 18:1–6). Churches committed to spiritual growth and effective witness will have a vital ministry of education to children.

A ministry of witness evangelism cannot be sustained in churches where education plays a minor role. People cannot witness to that which they know little about. Personal experience has an important place in Christian faith, but so does understanding. Scripture is quite explicit in calling us to love God with our minds as well as our hearts (Deuteronomy 6:5; Matthew 12:37; Mark 12:30; Luke 10:27). One of my mentors frequently reminded us that Christians needed to be able to outthink the world as well as outlive the world. Faith without knowledge is both impotent and dangerous. An effective witness to Jesus Christ thinks as well as feels and understands as well as believes.

STEP 10

Become a Gift-evoking Community

Spiritual gifts is one of those biblical phrases churches use but when pressed know very little about. Yet in the New Testament it is quite obvious that they are constitutive to the church's ministry. 1 Corinthians 12:4–11 is one example:

> Now there are varieties of gifts, but the same Spirit; and there are varieties of services, but the same Lord; and there are varieties of activities, but it is the same God who activates all of them in everyone. To each is given the manifestation of the Spirit for the common good. To one is given through the Spirit the utterance of wisdom, and to another the utterance of knowledge according to the same Spirit, to another faith by the same Spirit, to another gifts of healing by the one Spirit, to another the working of miracles, to another prophecy, to another the discernment of spirits, to another various kinds of tongues, to another the interpretation of tongues. All these are activated by one and the same Spirit, who allots to each one individually just as the Spirit chooses.

Ephesians 4:7, 11–13 is another example. It not only names five spiritual gifts but states their ultimate purpose:

> But each of us was given grace according to the measure of Christ's gift....The gifts he gave were that some would be apostles, some prophets, some evangelists, some pastors and teachers, to equip the saints for the work of ministry, for building up the body of Christ, until all of us come to the unity of the faith and of the knowledge of the Son of God, to maturity, to the measure of the full stature of Christ.

Romans 12:6–9 also mentions spiritual gifts:

> We have gifts that differ according to the grace given to us: prophecy, in proportion to faith; ministry, in

ministering; the teacher, in teaching; the exhorter, in exhortation; the giver, in generosity; the leader, in diligence; the compassionate, in cheerfulness. Let love be genuine; hate what is evil, hold fast to what is good.

1 Peter 4:10–11 says this about gifts:

Like good stewards of the manifold grace of God, serve one another with whatever gift each of you has received. Whoever speaks must do so as one speaking the very words of God; whoever serves must do so with the strength that God supplies, so that God may be glorified in all things through Jesus Christ. To him belong the glory and the power forever and ever. Amen.

More than twenty spiritual gifts are named in these three texts, some of them more than once. But there are others not named. There is no reason to think that Paul was trying to be anything other than suggestive. The Corinthian passage, for example, says there are various kinds of tongues but does not name them. Acts 2 refers to what is called *xenolalia* or speaking in other tongues, which is speaking under the Spirit in a way that allows people to listen in their native language. *Glossolalia*, or speaking in tongues, mentioned in Corinthians, means something quite different. It is speaking in a language known only to God, unless an interpreter is present. The diversity of tongues points to the general conclusion that spiritual gifts are both many and varied.

At the same time these passages define what a spiritual gift is only by implication. For a more definite meaning we need to look at the root word, which is *charis*. In the literal sense *charis* means a gracious act. In the scriptural context this gracious act means the divine influence upon the human heart that forms and shapes one's attitudes and actions. Thus, a spiritual gift can be understood as a particular way in which God's influence on the human heart finds expression. When the gift is evoked and exercised, it demonstrates gratitude for this influence.

We can see why these texts describe the church's ministry in terms of the exercising of the gifts of the Spirit. Whether it be apostleship, evangelism, teaching, prophecy, service, healing, preaching (exhorting), speaking in tongues, or any of the others, these ministries exist through gifts. As the Romans text says: "Prophecy, in proportion to faith; ministry, in [proportion to] ministering; the teacher, in [proportion to] teaching; the exhorter, in [proportion to] exhortation; the giver, in [proportion to] generosity; the leader, in [proportion to] diligence; the compassionate, in [proportion to] cheerfulness" (12:6–8).

Essential to understanding and even identifying spiritual gifts is the fact that they are given to the church. Gifts belong to the church, not to individuals. We are instruments of gifts. We do not possess them. Paul makes this clear in writing: "To each is given the manifestation of the Spirit for the common good" (1 Corinthians 12:7). In Ephesians he writes: "The gifts he gave were…to equip the saints for the work of ministry, for building up the body of Christ, until all of us come to the unity of the faith and of the knowledge of the Son of God, to maturity, to the measure of the full stature of Christ" (4:11–12). A spiritual gift builds and strengthens the church by equipping and nurturing others for their ministry. Thus, a spiritual gift always contributes to the common good. No spiritual gift exists for itself. It functions to create unity and wholeness for the body. Ministry builds ministry. That is why both the 1 Corinthians and Ephesians texts talk about spiritual gifts within the context of the "body" metaphor for the church. Gifts are like parts of the human body. They function to make the whole stronger and healthier. No part exists for itself. The role of a single gift, as with a single body part, is to serve the well-being of the entire body.

From this perspective churches engage in witness evangelism through the members' exercising spiritual gifts. In particular ways they demonstrate divine influence on the heart of a church as well as individual Christians. Over the years I have become convinced that each of us exercises one primary gift. We may be able to exercise multiple gifts, but a primary gift is always present and expresses itself through all the rest. Moreover, spiritual gifts are more than talents and abilities. These can be developed and fine-tuned. A seminary student, for example, can learn homiletical skills, but that does not give him the gift of preaching. Or she may learn what to do and not to do when visiting church members, but that does not give her the gift of pastoring. A person may learn music and be able to play an instrument, but that doesn't mean he has a musical gift. Some people can and do serve in leadership positions based on learned skills. Churches need these people. But the gift of leadership is more than learned skills. It has to do with vision casting, pointing direction, and inspiring confidence in others to follow. It has to do with nurturing others, moving a group of diverse and even contentious people toward clearly articulated goals. Not all people in leadership positions have this gift.

Talents and gifts are different. A talent may be the way in which a gift of the Spirit is exercised, but it is not the gift itself. Rather, the gift is the specific way the Spirit is present to reveal God's influence on our hearts. I think illustrations may be the most helpful way to explain what a spiritual gift is and is not.

Betty exercised the gift of hospitality. Meet her and you felt as if you had known her your whole life. She welcomed strangers into her life and made them instant friends. She was a woman you knew you could trust always to be real, always to want the best for you. I was once her pastor. I knew many of those who had shared that privilege before me. Each of us left that church knowing she was supportive of us, even when she might not have agreed with what we were doing. We knew she would never criticize us unfairly. If she wanted to say something, she came to us. She finally recognized her gift, and then invited anyone in the church to join her in a ministry of sharing the gift of hospitality. They formed a ministry group that focused on newcomers to the church and to those with special pastoral care needs. The small group

would meet on Monday morning, worship and study together, plan things they could do as part of their ministry,
pray for the people to be visited that week, and then depart
to go their separate ways to visit. Betty came alive in this
ministry because she was doing it, not out of a sense of duty
or obligation, but because it was the best way she knew to
exercise her gift of hospitality.

Laura exercises the spiritual gift of passion. Even in a
first meeting one is caught by her enthusiasm and energy
for her convictions. Intellectually bright, assertive without
being aggressive, and meticulous about details, her passion
is the way God's influence on her heart is seen, and it is irre-
sistibly contagious. She brings it to every task, whether it is
in her work as an educator or in her church chairing a committee or simply serving as one of its members. Moreover, it
attracts rather than overwhelms. Passion is the gift she exercises in all her leadership roles. That is how she builds up
the church. Not through what she can get a committee to do,
or how smoothly she can run a meeting. She builds the body
through her passion.

Roger exercises the spiritual gift of listening. Active in
his church, he enjoys a high level of trust among the members one would not expect to find with someone less than
forty years old. He is described as a man with a level head,
someone who knows people well and gets along with everyone. He seems to be the one to whom other leaders in his
church turn when there is a serious problem. But his gift is
listening. As one member put it: "Roger is somebody I think
everybody can talk to." That is a description of a person who
has the gift of listening. People trust him enough to talk to
him because they have found him to be a good listener. This
is the common denominator in the various leadership positions he has filled in his church through the years. It is the
way others experience the influence God has on Roger's
heart.

Dana exercises the spiritual gift of prophecy—not foresight, predicting the future, but insight, a capacity to see the

truth in a situation, to be able to have clearness about the issues at stake, and then to speak to others about those issues in a way that helps them see the truth as well. Though he is a multi-gifted man, my experience with Dana has convinced me his primary gift is prophecy. People are drawn to his preaching even though they know he will be provocative. But through his gift the Spirit awakens the truth in those who hear him. He is the kind of preacher who leads you to reevaluate all your values and priorities week after week and never feel condemned or "preached at." Other ministers can preach similar sermons and find themselves embroiled in controversy and division. But not Dana. He no doubt studied homiletics in seminary. He spends the necessary time good sermon preparation requires. It is obvious that he has learned the skills he needs for preaching. But none of these is his spiritual gift. It is through the exercising of his gift of prophecy that he builds up his church. This is the way others see God's influence on Dana's heart.

Gordon exercises the gift of discernment. For fifty years he has been able to lead his church to explore new lands and make tough decisions that would permanently change their collective life. He has known the right time for every movement in a new direction. He understands how important timing is in ministry, that one has to be able to read not only the signs but the "sighs" of the people to know where and when to lead them into uncharted waters. One also has to be able to distinguish between the praise of God and the praise of the crowd. Gordon has consistently done this. On more than one occasion he has chosen to move out of his comfort zone that had built up around a well-earned reputation for innovation and visionary leadership. He is courageous and insightful, prophetic and pastoral, but his primary gift is discernment.

These illustrations tell us that spiritual gifts are more than talents and abilities. They are the ways in which others see God's influence on our hearts, and on the heart of a congregation. Witness evangelism is the exercising of particular gifts in a particular ministry. Further, we know we are in the presence of a gift, not when it draws attention to the individual, but when it nurtures and strengthens the spiritual gifts of others, i.e., the whole church. No gift is more important than another because all build the church and, thus, all witness to Jesus Christ.

Becoming a gift-evoking community is the primary means by which mainline churches can tap the ministry of the laity. Gifts and call are inseparable in the life of the church because both are of the Spirit. Discerning the way in which we can use a spiritual gift helps to determine the ministry to which we are being called. Following a call sometimes helps us identify the spiritual gift we are to exercise. They work together.

The good news is that some mainline churches are at least talking about spiritual gifts. In one church I know the pastor conducts a class on the meaning of spiritual gifts on a regular basis, while the associate teaches classes on Christian spirituality. In another church the senior pastor has developed an entire curriculum focused on discovering spiritual gifts.[23] These are encouraging signs, but more is needed. The whole ministry of the church is at stake, but none more than intentional witness evangelism.

STEP 11

Focus on Baptism as the Laity's Call to Ministry

At the beginning of the chapter I noted that one of the most telling signs of spiritual stagnation is "church work" for laity. This step offers an alternative. There is no distinction between church members and church leaders in regard to ministry in the New Testament Gospels or the writings of the apostle Paul.[24] Baptism symbolizes the call of every church member into ministry. As we have already said, spiritual gifts have been given to all of us as members of the body of Christ. The ministry of witness evangelism demands of clergy a renewed commitment to equipping laity for their involvement in the church's ministry, not out of guilt or duty, but based on the call of Jesus Christ. This means much more than asking them to serve on a committee. That is little more than institutional maintenance in most churches. What is needed is for laity to trust that the same Spirit that empowers ministers will empower them. The only difference between the ordained and the laity lies in spiritual gifts, not in a call to ministry. All are called because all have been baptized.

The SLG process described earlier is an essential beginning for aiding laity in discerning their call to ministry. But other factors figure in this equipping of the saints, some of which place special responsibility on clergy leadership. One is creating an environment in which "No," as well as "Yes," becomes an appropriate answer in the church. The freedom to say Yes to a genuine call of God into ministry requires the freedom to say No to all the other voices that beckon us to follow. "Church work" rooted in institutional maintenance discourages laity in saying No when asked to serve. Thus they are never really free to say Yes to that which they truly feel led to do. Ministers need to encourage laity to say No as a way to set boundaries in making commitments. Most people have more demands on their time than they can meet. Doing ministry by call must not become another one on the list. Instead, church members have to learn the value and power of making it their first priority. This will require setting boundaries regarding one's commitments, both inside and outside the church. In the larger community it may mean turning down a leadership position in the PTA, the high school band boosters, the soccer league, a civic club, and a host of other invitations that come our way. In the church it may involve not singing in the choir, serving as a Sunday school teacher, class officer, member of a special committee, or chair of a church committee. All of these are important responsibilities, but they are to be done only as one senses a call to do them. Setting boundaries is not easy, but saying No paves the way for a genuine Yes. Once the freedom to say No has been established, then laity are ready to begin the demanding process of discerning a call to ministry. In many ways discerning a call is a trial and error kind of experience.

Another factor is helping laity recognize reliable signs of call. One of these is persistent nudges of the Holy Spirit, little promptings that come our way, sometimes quite unexpectedly, and do not leave us alone. One of the functions of prayer is to help us pay attention to these nudges. To share out of my own journey, this is precisely the way I felt the call to full-time ministry. As I was listening to someone read 1 Corinthians 13, I began to have this very strange thought that God wanted me in ministry. It seemed preposterous at the time, but the nudge wouldn't go away. A year later, as a college sophomore, I publicly declared my intention to enter the ministry. That is the way the Holy Spirit sometimes works.

Another sign of call is the sense that what one is being called to do is impossible. The task seems too formidable for us. The call story of Gideon (Judges 6:1–40) is a marvelous example of this. The task was impossible, but Gideon responded anyway. Abraham must have felt the same way, as did Moses, David, Jeremiah, Peter, and Paul. The Bible is one story after another of God calling people to do the impossible and their initial resistance to answering Yes. Is it any wonder that Jesus had this encounter with his own disciples?

> The disciples were perplexed at these words. But Jesus said to them again, "Children, how hard it is to enter the kingdom of God! It is easier for a camel to go through the eye of a needle than for someone who is rich to enter the kingdom of God." They were greatly astounded, and said to one another, "Then who can be saved?" Jesus looked at them and said, "For mortals it is impossible, but not for God; for God all things are possible." (Mark 10:24–27)

We are not called to follow an easy or hard way. We are called to follow the way God wants us to go. At times that may appear being called to do the impossible. Our responsibility is not to make that judgment, but to trust that if it is a genuine call to ministry, the way will be shown to us.

A third reliable sign of call is the recognizing that what we feel called to do will require personal sacrifice. Ministry is hard. As one person put it, "Every day it gets harder and harder, and better and better." The "better" cannot be separated from the "hard" part. This is the "It doesn't make any sense" dimension of discerning call. Giving up a successful career to enter ministry makes no sense, yet people continue to do it. Moving to a small town in the middle of nowhere after living comfortably in the suburbs of a large city makes no sense, but people continue to do it for the sake of ministry. Getting up at 6:00 in the morning to join a group whose ministry will be working with the poorest of the poor in your city makes no sense, but I know people who have done it anyway. Ministry involves time, money, energy, maybe a radical change in lifestyle, certainly a change in attitude. Avoiding sacrifice is not an option in doing ministry. It is one way we know God is calling.

The wisdom and perspective of others is yet another reliable sign in discerning call. It is the nature of being the body of Christ that we help each other discern a call to ministry. There are no "Lone Rangers" in ministry. Just as spiritual gifts are given to the church, so is the ministry of Jesus Christ. Our ministry is one part of that which is larger than any one of us alone. Within community it is often one person speaking to another person about a ministry that helps that person discern a call. When I went off to college, my hometown pastor asked me what I planned to study and then said that he was hoping I might enter the ministry. Had he not said that I might have missed the Spirit's nudging when it came. He planted the seed.

Listening to students sharing their spiritual autobiographies, I am always impressed by the frequency of their mentioning someone who spoke to them about entering ministry before the thought had come to them. The church as the body of Christ can do this for all its members. It is not just that individuals serve the good of the community. The community is to serve the good of the individuals. Helping one another hear a call to ministry is one way this happens.

Finally, the study and praying of scripture always provide assistance in the discernment of call. The Bible is filled with stories of the call of God on the lives of people just as human and frail as we are. One of the most basic lessons in all of them is that we are dependent on God to do any ministry. What laity need to know is that an awareness of our own inadequacies is a reliable sign that we are finally getting the message straight. Their feelings of inadequacy in the face of something they think God might be calling them to do position them to discern the truth of the call with greater confidence. What clergy need to teach laity is that it is our inadequacies in the face of the great challenges ministries place before us that make following any call a courageous step and a sure sign that we are being called by God to do it.

These signs of call do not guarantee clear discernment, but they do offer a practical way to ask and trust that we shall receive, seek and trust that we shall find, knock and trust the door will be opened to us (Matthew 7:7). The important thing is that the process itself is spiritually enriching and significantly increases the possibility that laity will begin doing the ministries they genuinely feel called to do.

+ + + + +

The above steps offer mainline churches a practical way to reclaim evangelism by helping them confront the primary obstacle to it. Intentional witnessing depends on the church being the church, living out of a deep center of spiritual power, functioning as the body of Christ engaged in ministries that witness to the One who is the head. It is a minstry that embodies the conviction that "the most credible form of witness (and the most effective thing it can do for the world) is the actual creation of a living, breathing, visible community of faith."[25]

NOTES

[1] A men's movement founded by Bill McCartney, the former football coach at Colorado State University, that sponsors gatherings for Christian men featuring top name speakers, prayer vigils, and workshops. Promise Keepers has gained worldwide attention, primarily because of its ability to draw thousands of men to their events.

[2] Jean Vanier, *From Brokenness to Community.* (See note 32, ch. 2.)

[3] Ibid., p. 233.

[4] Abraham Joshua Heschel, *The Sabbath: Its Meaning for Modern Man* (New York: The Noonday Press, 1951), p. 13.

[5] Ibid., p. 6.

[6] Dorothy C. Bass, "Keeping Sabbath," *Practicing Our Faith: A Way of Life for a Searching People* (San Francisco: Jossey-Bass, 1997), p. 81.

[7] The sermon was delivered at the General Assembly of the Christian Church (Disciples of Christ) gathered in Pittsburgh, Pennsylvania, October 20–24, 1995.

[8] See the selected bibliography in *The Jesus Connection* for suggestions.

[9] See my book *Christians Must Choose: The Lure of Culture and the Command of Christ* (St. Louis: CBP Press, 1981).

[10] *Resident Aliens* (Nashville: Abingdon, 1989), p. 119.

[11] James C. Collins and Jerry I. Porras, *Built To Last: Successful Habits of Visionary Companies* (New York: HarperCollins, 1997), pp. 46–90.

[12] Ibid., p. 81.

[13] This is clearly the conclusion the Barna Research Group reached in their study of numerically growing churches, *Successful Churches: What They Have in Common*, p. 30 (See note 15, ch. 1). In a lecture delivered on our campus September 25, 1997, Dr. Beau Weston, Assistant Professor of Sociology at Center College, Danville, Kentucky, asserted that churches need to have "a barrier to entrance and exit," by which he meant that churches needed to make membership's worth people entering and not leaving. His lecture was based on an article he wrote entitled "The Religion Market," available in an abridged version from Center College Public Relations Office and in the longer version published in the Kentucky Humanities (1997, No. 1) by the Kentucky Humanities Council, 206 E. Maxwell Street, Lexington, KY 40508.

[14] *Worship Evangelism*, p. 42. (See note 1, ch. 3.)

[15] Collins and Porras, *Built To Last*, pp. 43–45. (See note 11 above.)

[16] Ibid., pp. 52–53.

[17] Morgenthaler, p. 30. (See note 1, ch. 3.)

[18] James Emery Whites, *Opening the Front Door: Worship and Church Growth* (Nashville: Convention, 1992), pp. 19–20. Always asking for money was number one.

[19] See Morgenthaler (note 1, ch. 3) for a discussion of the long term value of these attempts in attracting baby boomers (Chapter 1).

[20] From an article entitled "Preaching, A Spiritual Act" by Larry Paul Jones, *The Lexington Quarterly*, 31:4, Winter 1996, p. 282.

[21] John Westerhoff, "Evangelism, Evangelization, and Catechesis," *Interpretation*, 48:2, April, 1994.

[22] See Dean Kelley, *Why Conservative Churches are Growing,* and Hoge, Johnson, and Luidens, *Vanishing Boundaries* (see note 16, ch. 1).

[23] For this material, write Paul Smith, Broadway Baptist Church, 3931 Washington St., Kansas City, MO 64111. See also Thomas R. Hawkins, *Claiming God's Promises: A Guide to Discovering Your Spiritual Gifts* (Nashville: Abingdon, 1992), and Gary L. Harbaugh, *God's Gifted People* (Minneapolis: Augsburg, 1988).

[24] See Eugene Bartlett, *Ministry in the New Testament* (Minneapolis: Augsburg Fortress, 1993).

[25] *Resident Aliens,* p. 47.

5

Restructuring for Witness Evangelism

We have talked about the meaning and theological foundation for intentional witness evangelism. We have discussed the problem of spiritual stagnation that prevents congregations from becoming witnessing churches and identified specific steps that can be taken to confront it. But the truth is, nothing will really change in mainline churches unless and until there is a major restructuring of their organizational life. There is an inseparable and indispensable relationship between Spirit and structure in the body of Christ. Structures are not neutral. They either enhance or inhibit ministry. They serve or hinder the work of the Spirit. As Jean Vanier has said:

> The essence of the challenge to a growing community is to adapt its structures so that they can go on enabling the growth of individuals and not simply conserve the tradition, still less a form of authority and a prestige.

These days, we tend to see spirit and structure as being in opposition to each other. The challenge is to create structures which serve the spirit and the growth of people and which are themselves nourishing.[1]

Then he makes the startling comment:

Structures are...the mirrors of the heart.[2]

That's it! Structures are mirrors of the heart, or at least can be. They can be extensions of our devotion and commitment. They can embody our passions, reveal our hearts, show what's important to us. They can show the world where our treasure is. Jesus tried to tell us this when he said:

No one sews a piece of unshrunk cloth on an old cloak, for the patch pulls away from the cloak, and a worse tear is made. Neither is new wine put into old wineskins; otherwise, the skins burst, and the wine is spilled, and the skins are destroyed; but new wine is put into fresh wineskins, and so both are preserved.
(Matthew 9:16–17)

If structures can be called "mirrors of the heart," then it stands to reason that present-day church structures ought to reflect the best of what is in the hearts of contemporary Christians. In other words, if we truly desire to witness to our own conversion to Jesus Christ as Savior and Lord, then the way the church is organized ought to facilitate this ministry. Certainly a change in organization will not solve the problems mainline churches are facing. But it is naive for mainline church leaders and members to think structures have little impact on our capacity to witness. Indeed, the impact is profound and, I believe, at the present time mostly negative. Current structures not only do little to help churches manifest the fruit of the Spirit, evoke and exercise spiritual gifts, or assist laity in discerning their call to ministry; they actually inhibit this from happening.

Ironically, mainline churches have failed to learn what growth churches have known for a long time—structure is supposed to serve ministry, not vice versa. The Barna Research Group found that numerically growing churches accepted the fact that "ministry is not called to fit the church's structure, rather the structure exists to further effective ministry." Further, that "structure was viewed as a support system, a means to an end, rather than an end in itself."[3] Structures always influence the life and spirit of the people who live within them.

Perhaps a brief history lesson can put the current situation in perspective. In general, whether a congregation is part of a connectional system, such as the United Methodist Church, or has congregational autonomy, such as the Christian Church (Disciples of Christ), a business model of organization governs the church at all levels. Its origins date from the late 1940s. This approach viewed the church from a business perspective, albeit a "Christian" one. One influential book at the time put it this way:

> The church is a divine business in which there is an intimate partnership. One Partner is the source of unfailing wisdom, the supply of inexhaustible resources, a Companion of enriching personality, and a sharer of overflowing power. The other partner, equally essential to the enterprise, is the source of talent, time, energy, money and personality. Guided by the mind and spirit of the Senior Partner, this junior partner serves as steward of all the stock of the church and is the administrator of its affairs. The success of the business will depend upon the energy, the integrity, and the vision of the junior partner. The Senior Partner never fails. His resources and his energy are never lacking.[4]

The images are clear enough. The world of business became the point of reference for the life of the church. The goal was to enable the church to become as efficient and effective as a well-run business. The minister was the CEO and the members the workers. Governing boards, committees, and departments were formed to facilitate the church's work. Without questioning the motives or impugning the integrity of those who promoted this functional structure for the church, I am convinced the long-term effects of using a business model of organization have been devastating. Effectiveness in the church is now measured not only by growth, but by organizational efficiency and cost effectiveness. In many instances ministry has become limited to anticipated revenues, and risking to follow what is perceived to be a call of God is often criticized as impractical and imprudent; in short, not good business. Worst of all, lay ministry is now understood almost exclusively as serving the organizational and maintenance needs of the church.

Yet this is not even the worst effect of the business-model approach to church. More damaging has been its basic presupposition that ministry can be programmed. This is what I call a "needs assessment" view of ministry. A need is identified and a program is developed to meet it. Success is determined by the number, and on occasion the quality, of programs being generated and sustained. The assumption at work is that the greater the number of programs, the greater the number of needs being met. As interest in one program declines, a new one is generated, most often at the initiative of the ministerial staff. Almost without exception, though commitment is desired, programmed ministry survives by congregational participation on the basis of personal interest. On occasion an individual may make a long-term commitment to a program, such as a Habitat for Humanity project, but on the whole such involvement is limited to a few. The majority participate on a sporadic basis, depending upon their level of interest and/or desire to support their church.

To be fair, the business model has led churches to develop many worthwhile programs to meet needs that have

cried out for attention. But in this process spiritual nurture
has been modest. Worse, mild religion has become the most
the church can hope for. Expectations for membership are
driven by what people are willing to give rather than what
the gospel demands. Yielding to a consumeristic environment, churches devote time and energy to promotionalism,
as if they have a product to sell rather than a mission to fulfill. It is not surprising that people outside the church see it
as simply one among many organizations trying to do good
things. Because the business model dominates the church
today, a worst-case scenario for the ministry of witness evangelism would be for mainline churches to think of it as another program to try.[5]

Another Way to Structure the Church

I believe overcoming the state of spiritual stagnation will
require the restructuring of mainline church life. Too many
mainline ministers and church members are weary and worn
down by the weight of the institutional bureaucracy that has
built up around the business model of church. Thus, without restructure, the ministry of witness evangelism will be
viewed as another program to be done by the active minority who are already tired and discouraged at having to do
everything. That there is a faithful minority doing the majority of the work stems from the disease of spectatorship.
Most church members who actually attend church fall into
this category. Their involvement seldom extends beyond
worship. They attend but do not attend to the life of the
church. Dietrich Bonhoeffer once wrote:

> In Christian community everything depends upon
> whether each individual is an indispensable link in a
> chain. Only when even the smallest link is securely
> interlocked is the chain unbreakable. A community
> which allows unemployed members to exist within
> it will perish because of them.[6]

"Unemployed" members are not bad people, nor even uncommitted people. They are often people who have never had any help in discovering the gift of the Spirit they can exercise (see Step 10) or finding their call to ministry (Step 11). They have been allowed to sit and watch.

What follows is a detailed description of a way to facilitate people's moving from being spectators to becoming full participants in their congregation's life and ministry. It would be impossible to anticipate all the particularities that will affect restructuring. Thus, no prescription is intended here. The idea is simply to describe in appropriate detail how churches can move to a new structure for ministry. Each congregation will have to adapt this process to make it work for itself.

The approach to ministry I am suggesting as an alternative to the business model of church is the rather uncomplicated but very demanding structure that I call "ministry groups."[7] Ministry groups naturally flow out of the kind of Spiritual Life Groups described in the previous chapter. The structure consists of small groups that have a threefold purpose: (1) to embody the laity's call to ministry through a commitment to a specific ministry; (2) to stay connected to Jesus through a disciplined spiritual life that includes prayer, spiritual journaling, Bible reading and Bible study, and any other spiritual disciplines individual groups may decide can be helpful; and (3) to focus attention on the witnessing nature of the ministry around which the group has gathered. Essential to ministry groups functioning around this threefold purpose is the establishment of a group covenant to which the members commit themselves. The covenant should include at least the following elements: (1) regular attendance to ministry group meetings; (2) daily practice of spiritual disciplines; (3) ministry group worship time in every meeting; (4) education about the area of ministry in which the group is serving; (5) sharing ultimate responsibility for the health and well-being of the group's life and ministry; and (6) working on behalf of the group ministry. What this does is to keep focus on the integrity of group membership. Other aspects of the covenant may be added, but experience has shown that the ones named above are basic.

Also important to the integrity of group life is a process of accountability for the covenant. One way is to spend time each meeting talking about how each group member is working at keeping faith with the group covenant. Another way is to have members turn in weekly, bi-weekly, or monthly written spiritual reflections to a person in the group who has the gift of spiritual direction. The spiritual director returns the reflections at the next meeting with comments intended to offer guidance and encouragement. Students in my spiritual formation classes do this on a weekly basis. They indicate that it is a helpful process that keeps them disciplined and aids in their growth and development. Accountability in some form is indispensable in ministry groups. At the least it highlights the fact that it takes TEAM (Time, Energy, Attention, Money) for a group to live out its call to ministry.

Typically a ministry group stays together for one year, at which time it dissolves in order to release the members to recommit or to join a different ministry. Whether a new group is formed depends upon whether anyone senses a call to renew the covenant. Also important is for members to agree that withdrawal from the group will be done in conversation with the other members. This way anyone who leaves will do so with the group's blessing, support, and prayers. Finally, time, place, and frequency of group meetings are ultimately determined by the ministry group, but initially these are set by the person first sounding the call for the ministry.

Obviously the adoption of the ministry group approach is not something that a congregation will do overnight. The old business model will continue to exist and make its demands during any transition time. The congregational sabbatical will help with this, especially in the establishment of spiritual life groups that educate people on the fruit and gifts of the Spirit, as well as other issues I have raised. But vestiges of the old structure will remain for some time. Let me suggest what experience has shown to be a way to make this transition easier than it would otherwise be.

First, traditional committees or departments such as education, mission, community action, nurture, worship, youth, and others are restructured as "ministries." This is more than a name change. Members join these ministries based on a sense of call rather than by being appointed or persuaded to participate. The work involved (prayer and action) is made clear in the first meeting, and only those willing to make the commitment return to the next meeting. Experience has shown that new ministries emerge once the ministry group structure is in place, but initially the traditional areas can serve as a launching pad to this new approach. Second, an existing group in the church composed of clergy and laity (cabinet, board, session, nominating committee) identifies those church members whom they discern to be persons who could serve effectively as moderators of the various ministries. The candidates are asked to serve, with sufficient time to pray and think before responding. It is important that the person being asked understand that she is free to say No. Any ministry for which no moderator is found does not function until one emerges. Third, all church members are then invited to pray about where they believe God is calling them to serve in the next year and then sign up for that ministry. Once the ministry groups are formed, they begin their life together.

Once ministry groups begin to function, a ministry council consisting of moderators from the various ministries is formed. The council has three purposes:

(1) *Communication.* It is important for all ministries to know what each one is doing. This makes scheduling simpler, but more importantly, it is a way for one group to offer intercessory prayer on behalf of the others.

(2) *Sanctioning of all new ministry groups.* A process needs to be developed by which the body as a whole holds each group accountable to embody the core beliefs and values of

the whole body. No single group should go running off on its own without regard to how it affects the rest of the body or fits into the larger vision the church has for its total ministry. When a church member senses a call to a ministry that is not already established, he shares the call with the council, invites affirmation, and then respects the council's wisdom in supporting or not supporting the ministry. This is another dimension of accountability built into the ministry group structure that avoids any temptation for one to become a Lone Ranger minister.

(3) *Allocation of ministry funding.* In the business model, the finance or stewardship committee establishes a budget for each committee based upon requests made. Then the committee tries to stay within that budget for the year. I call this doing ministry by budget. In the ministry group approach, the stewardship ministry, in consultation with all the ministries and ministerial staff and with approval from the governing body, establishes a total amount of ministry money, excluding yearly administrative and property costs, and denominational support. The council divides that amount by twelve and then invites each ministry to request monthly allotments. If the monthly amount is insufficient for what a ministry needs, its representative can request the council to set aside more than one month's sum for this purpose.

Essential to the council's work is that all decisions be made by consensus, as described in Chapter 5. Having had personal experience with this approach, I found it to be an effective process for the distribution of financial support for the different ministries of a church. Part of the reason it worked so well is that reasons for budget requests were carefully thought through by the individual ministries and the council. Each ministry became much more knowledgeable about all the others, and the sense of ownership for the ministry in which one was serving increased. It is a process that works.

One question often raised about this structure is the relationship of the ministry council to the governing body of the church. Perhaps a representative or two from the council might serve on this body, along with the other designated members such as elders, deacons, and others representing groups in the church. In other words, the council does not take the place of an official governing body. It is, rather, similar to what is often called "the church cabinet." Again, the change in language is more than semantic, but comparisons may help to clarify how the council functions in relationship to existing groups.

Another question is whether the ministry group structure has any place for committees. The answer is Yes, with qualifications. Committees are defined as a specific group with a specific task of limited duration. The clergy/laity leader development group mentioned earlier, for example, could be formed into a permanent committee meeting once a year to identify ministry moderators. Other short-term tasks may be handled by committees, such as the search for additional staff, special events, or celebrations. Once the task is complete, the committee ceases to function. A task force might be a more appropriate name for such groups. The point is that they are short term.

The ministry group structure makes no apology for its call to a deep level of commitment among church members. Nor is it naive about what is involved. Reordering previous time commitments may be required initially. But what is at stake is following the call of God on a person's life, which is why ministry group membership should not be entered into out of a sense of duty, guilt, or obligation. These provide no solid foundation for making ministry our primary commitment in life. Only the call of God can empower us to do that. It is what keeps ministers in the ministry. It is what will keep the laity in ministry as well.

Ministry groups, then, are the heart and soul of the ministry of witness evangelism because they are the specific points of collective witness for the body of Christ. The ministry may be to the church or in the world. Legitimate needs exist in both places. What matters is that every ministry group see itself as a collective witness to Jesus in the world, grounded in the conviction that when groups gather around a common call to ministry, they will begin to have the time of their lives in ministry. There will be struggles and problems because people are people. But by the very nature of them, ministry groups make such struggles worth it.

The Leadership Key

The most important issue mainline churches face today is clergy leadership. It is the key to everything else. If effective witness evangelism depends upon restructuring congregations, the latter depends upon good clergy leadership.[8] The word "competent" may seem more appropriate, but the word is generally associated with knowledge and skills. "Good," on the other hand, goes further than competence by suggesting character as a major component of leadership. Competence with character is the meaning of the term "good" being used in this context. Mainline churches desperately need good ministerial leadership if spiritual renewal is to take place. I want to identify specifically what this kind of leadership actually means in the life of a church.

My thinking is influenced by the writings of Robert Greenleaf, who worked for AT&T for thirty-seven years in a position that can be described as "a paid thinker." During these years Greenleaf developed the concept of "the servant leader" that became his life's work. A Quaker by faith, Greenleaf believed that the kind of leadership all institutions needed was persons who had the desire first and foremost to be a servant. Servanthood meant attending to the "highest priority needs" of others, needs he defined as "growing as persons, becoming healthier, wiser, freer, more autonomous, more likely themselves to become servants." Further, he said, in the process of serving the highest priority needs of those the leader is leading, "the least privileged persons in society will either benefit, or, at least, not be further deprived. No one will be knowingly hurt, directly or indirectly."[9]

But Greenleaf didn't stop with servanthood. A servant leader not only wants first to be a servant. She also makes the choice to lead. For Greenleaf this meant "being able to point direction better than most," what he called "foresight," or the ability to provide the vision that determines the direction a group follows. The leader must also be able to articulate this vision or direction with clarity in order to gain the trust of those being led. Empathetic listening, the capacity for genuine caring, the recognition of one's own weaknesses, a serious commitment to prayer—all of these are part of servant leadership in Greenleaf's thinking. But what stands out in his work is the need for leaders to lead, to be bold and confident in pointing direction. If one truly has the desire deep inside to serve first, then leading in this way can be done without becoming arrogant or conceited.

More than "teacher," "resident theologian," "reflective practitioner," or other descriptions of clergy leadership today, I suggest that "servant-leader" is the most encompassing term available. It strikes the necessary balance between the desire to serve and the choice to lead. Greenleaf understood ministry as a vocation, a calling, rather than a job. But he also was acutely aware of the need for leaders who want to serve the needs of others to be able to provide guidance and direction for those being led, especially in large groups or institutions. He was convinced that without the capacity to act with foresight, a leader is a leader in name only. Worse, as events start forcing the person's hand, leadership becomes little more than reacting to immediate events.[10]

Dreaming great dreams is also a part of foresight. Greenleaf often said that nothing happened without a dream, and nothing great happened without a great dream. Dreaming dreams calls for taking risks. The servant-leader is one who has the capacity to articulate the direction to follow with such clearness that others catch it and become willing to take the necessary risks to achieve it. He was not an advocate of quick fixes or revolutionary changes, but he believed that playing it safe was no behavior for a person or institution wanting to serve the highest priority needs of others.

Jean Vanier echoes what Greenleaf says about servant leadership when he writes:

> Leaders of a community have a double mission. They must keep their eyes and those of the community on what is essential, on the fundamental aims of the community. They must give direction, so that the community doesn't get lost in small wrangles, which are secondary and incidental.[11]

Further,

> The role of any leader is to help each member to reflect more personally, to discern and make wise decisions and assume responsibility. A leader must call each one to growth [in love and truth].[12]

This is the kind of clergy leadership mainline churches need today, leaders who want to serve and are able to point direction better than most in the life of the church; leaders who have a passion for the gospel, who do not have to be convinced to lead churches into witnessing ministries but, rather, cannot be kept from it; leaders who know ministers are not managers, administrators, or manipulators of resources; leaders who have the courage to make decisions, who trust in God in spite of not having all the answers, who desire to seek the reign of God in all aspects of life and, thus, are unafraid to be seekers after justice; leaders who possess sufficient intellectual strength to see the road ahead and who have the spiritual character, in the words of Rudyard Kipling, to keep their heads when everyone else is losing theirs and blaming it on you.[13]

It will take this kind of leadership to stem the tide of spiritual stagnation among mainliners, to bring focus to living by the fruit and gifts of the Spirit, and to teach laity to discern and follow their call to ministries that by their very nature make a witness to the name of Jesus. Greenleaf may have summed up the need for this kind of leadership in mainline churches when he pointedly observed:

> As I get about churches and church-related institutions, I am impressed by the extent to which they employ commercial consultants to advise them and by the presence in their work of procedures I would label as gimmicks. Both, it seems to me, are evidences of inadequate religious leadership.[14]

Nothing, absolutely nothing, can substitute for clergy servant leadership in mainline churches. Say what we will about lay leadership in the church, the role of the clergy remains the key to the effectiveness of any congregation's life and witness. The very leadership of the laity depends upon it. The need is not for charismatic leaders. They come and go, leaving in the wake both good and bad. Servant leaders are what mainline churches need. They are the ones who will lead the church into the twenty-first century.

But where will they come from? How will God raise them up? I suggest that our role in answering these questions is to renew the covenantal partnership between mainline churches and their seminaries. Seminaries need churches that prayerfully discern those within their community who demonstrate a capacity for ministry and then nurture the potential for call that might be there. The body of Christ must once again become proactive in Jesus' calling people into ministry. Ananias's role in Paul's understanding what happened to him on the Damascus Road as a call to ministry (Acts 9) is paradigmatic for the church.

The other side of the partnership means churches need seminaries to educate the men and women they send to become leaders. Seminaries focus their energies around teaching students to think biblically, theologically, globally, inclusively, and rightly so. But churches also need them to graduate people who are servant leaders, who have people skills, spiritual maturity, and foresight to point direction. The "how to's" of ministry are not what is lacking in seminary education. Educating persons to become servant leaders who can help those being served to grow into spiritually mature Christians is what is lacking. All the skills and techniques in the world cannot do this. People who are committed to their own calls to discipleship and ministry, who know the fruit and gifts of the Spirit in their own lives, who can think biblically and theologically about skills, people whom the church joyfully affirms for ministry, these are the leaders seminaries and churches together need to educate and nurture.

Good leaders. Servant leaders. The indispensable element in any group's life. In the current environment of mainline church life today, it is not an overstatement to say that everything written here comes down to this: The witness of any church will be enhanced or inhibited by the quality of its clergy leadership. May God send, may the church raise up, may the Holy Spirit empower good leaders for declining mainline churches who can point the way to becoming winsome witnesses to the gospel of Jesus Christ.

NOTES

[1] Jean Vanier, *Community and Growth* (New York: Paulist Press, 1989), p. 108.

[2] Ibid., p. 308.

[3] *Successful Churches*, p. 30. (See note 15, ch. 1.)

[4] O. L. Shelton, *The Church Functioning Effectively* (St. Louis: Christian Board of Publication, 1946), p. 15.

[5] As a teacher of spiritual formation for many years, I have been dismayed to see the current interest in spirituality take precisely this turn. To a significant degree denominational executives are responsible for this trend. They seem to want to "package" everything into a program in the name of making it more "accessible" to all churches.

[6] Dietrich Bonhoeffer, *Life Together* (New York: Harper & Row, 1954), p. 94.

[7] Ministry Groups are adapted from the "mission group" structure used by the Church of the Savior in Washington, D.C. I am indebted to this community for its influence on me and my understanding of church during the last twenty-five years. I owe a similar debt to my former mentor, Dr. Elton Trueblood, who first exposed me to the concept of small disciplined

groups in the church as a strategy for "penetrating" the world with the gospel through witness.

[8] See Callahan's argument for the "missionary pastor" concept of leadership over against the "professional minister" concept that focuses on church maintenance (*Effective Church Leadership: Building on the Twelve Keys*, San Francisco: Harper & Row, 1990). Also, a helpful book on leadership in today's church is *The Responsibility People*, edited by William McKinney (Eerdmans Publishing Company, 1994). It consists of essays and interviews with eighteen senior leaders of Protestant churches and national ecumenical agencies, most of whom are retired. The material reflects a wide range of experience and knowledge from leaders whose love for and commitment to the continuing vitality of mainline churches is winsome, and whose views on what makes for good leadership in the church are pastoral, yet provocative.

[9] Robert K. Greenleaf, "Religious leaders as Seekers and Servants," *Seeker and Servant: The Private Writings of Robert Greenleaf*, Anne T. Fraker & Larry C. Spears, ed. (San Francisco: Jossey-Bass Publishers, 1996), p. 40.

[10] Ibid.

[11] *Community and Growth*, pp. 212–213. (See note 1 above.)

[12] Ibid., p. 292.

[13] The poem "If," in Rudyard Kipling, *Gunga Din and Other Favorite Poems* (New York: Dover Publications, Inc., 1990), p. 59.

[14] *Seeker and Servant*, p. 33. (See note 9 above.)